The
Mindful
Investor

*How a Calm Mind
Can Bring You Inner Peace
and Financial Security*

The Mindful Investor

How a Calm Mind Can Bring You Inner Peace and Financial Security

Maria Gonzalez, MBA & Graham Byron, CFP

John Wiley & Sons Canada, Ltd.

Care has been taken to trace ownership of copyright material contained in this book. The publisher will gladly receive any information that will enable them to rectify any reference or credit line in subsequent editions.

Graham Byron is an Investment Advisor with CIBC Wood Gundy in Toronto. CIBC Wood Gundy is a division of CIBC World Markets Inc., a subsidiary of CIBC and Member CIPF. The views expressed in this book are those of the authors, and do not necessarily reflect those of CIBC World Markets Inc.

Calculations and projections included in the text are for demonstration purposes only. They are based on a number of assumptions and consequently actual results may differ, possibly to a material degree. Readers are advised to seek advice regarding their particular circumstances from their personal financial, tax, and legal advisors.

Library and Archives Canada Cataloguing in Publication Data

Gonzalez, Maria, 1958–
    The mindful investor : how a calm mind can bring you inner peace and financial security / Maria Gonzalez, Graham Byron.

Includes index.
ISBN 978-0-470-73766-8

    1. Finance, Personal—Religious aspects. 2. Finance, Personal—Psychological aspects. 3. Meditation. I. Byron, Graham. II. Title.

HG4527.G66 2009   332.024'01   C2009-905474-4

Production Credits
Cover design: Pat Loi
Interior design and typesetting: Pat Loi
Cover image: iStockphoto.com
Printer: Friesens

John Wiley & Sons Canada, Ltd.
6045 Freemont Blvd.
Mississauga, Ontario
L5R 4J3

Printed in Canada

1 2 3 4 5 FP 13 12 11 10 09

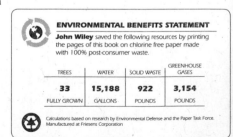

ENVIRONMENTAL BENEFITS STATEMENT
John Wiley saved the following resources by printing the pages of this book on chlorine free paper made with 100% post-consumer waste.

TREES	WATER	SOLID WASTE	GREENHOUSE GASES
33	**15,188**	**922**	**3,154**
FULLY GROWN	GALLONS	POUNDS	POUNDS

Calculations based on research by Environmental Defense and the Paper Task Force.
Manufactured at Friesens Corporation

To Gaetano, my soulmate, for his unconditional love, support, and clarity.

To my mother, Alvarina, for her compassion, encouragement, and inspiration.

And to Peanut, for teaching me through his mindfulness.

—Maria Gonzalez

To Diana. I love you, and appreciate your (almost) unwavering patience every day.

And to my girls, Gillian, Mary, and Lizzie. You're the best, I'm so proud of you all.

—Graham Byron

Table of Contents

Acknowledgments

Maria would like to thank:

Shinzen Young, my teacher, for his compassion and wisdom. I am deeply grateful for his coaching, his encouragement of my practice and my teaching, and his unconditional support. This book could not have been written without his innovative Mindfulness techniques, which have made the 2,500-year-old science of the mind accessible to our contemporary culture.

A number of Shinzen's teachings are contained and cited in chapter 2, and some of his techniques are described in chapter 3. You can view him on YouTube on the Expansion & Contraction channel, and visit his website at www.basicmindfulness.org.

My husband, Gaetano Geretto, for his advice, encouragement, and meticulous proofing, and for always putting things in perspective. I am deeply grateful for his grace and mindfulness throughout the writing process.

Soryu Scott, for being such a mindful sounding board and for his mindful decision-making algorithm, which appears in appendix A. It's a very innovative and useful tool for making mindful decisions. You can visit his website at www.budsa.org.

Graham, for suggesting we co-write this book. He is an exemplary student of Mindfulness, and it's my pleasure and privilege to work with him. He is also the quintessential mindful advisor.

Graham would like to thank:

Maria. She is an ideal teacher, coach, and guide. One of my goals is to emulate the way she conducts her life and runs her business.

And we both would like to thank:

Diana Byron, for her flawless editing, support, and terrific sense of humour. She kept us on track throughout the writing process. She had an unwavering can-do attitude, and this book could not have been published without her.

The entire team at Wiley. Particular thanks go to Karen Milner, Senior Editor, for her support, flexibility, and encouragement, and to Jennifer Smith, Vice President & Publisher, for believing in our project and encouraging us to write this book. She understood that these times require an alternative mindset and innovative strategies, and knew that it would benefit readers to hear our message.

Preface

Money. The word itself has a power of its own. It can induce feelings and start a train of thought instantly. Unfortunately, often these feelings and thoughts are negative and stressful. We believe that achieving a healthy relationship with money is necessary because it's attached, in some way, to almost every aspect of our lives. In reality most people have enough money, even after the recent market collapse. What they don't have is the level of calm, clarity, focus, and equanimity required to live peacefully with money. Mindfulness can help achieve it. We will focus a great deal on equanimity throughout the book, and while the term may seem unfamiliar, it simply means accepting your thoughts and feelings without judgment, which allows you to maintain balance.

The Mindful Investor is a friendly, non-threatening guide for individual investors, business people, and professionals who are looking for a better way to manage their money. We believe that financial success is important, but we believe that you must create your own definition of success, and this will vary for everyone. We'll assist you in creating your definition by guiding you to achieve clarity about what's truly important to you, and showing you how to stay focused on what matters and be equanimous with what you can't control.

The tool we will introduce you to is Mindfulness meditation. The benefits of Mindfulness meditation in the worlds of business and finance include:

- Greater focus and concentration
- Improved time management
- An enhanced ability to anticipate and serve client needs
- Enhanced team effectiveness
- Greater innovation and inspiration
- Increased productivity
- More clarity about what matters, including financial goals
- A sense of equanimity, or acceptance of what you can't control, and an end to worrying about money

We begin with a brief overview of the financial crises experienced over the course of 2007 to 2009, and will demonstrate to you the applicability and helpfulness of Mindfulness meditation in coping with the current disarrayed economy. Next we introduce you to Mindfulness meditation—its history, applications, and benefits. You should feel reassured that it's relatively easy, secular, mainstream, and accessible to everyone who's interested. Once you've comfortably settled in, we'll explore some of the simpler methods of practising Mindfulness in everyday life and help you get started on your journey. We'll also introduce you to five hindrances to success, so you can be aware of them and sidestep potential disasters relating to them.

Many personal finance books focus on giving up lattes and dining out for the purposes of saving up your pennies for retirement. This isn't one of them. We focus on the big picture. And the first step in creating financial success is to define what financial success means for you.

We teach you how to employ Mindfulness in order to become clear about your true goals, and we point out frequent pitfalls and provide suggestions for avoiding them. We'll walk you through the components of a typical financial plan and offer advice on what to consider when answering the questions that form the basis of a plan. Once you're armed with a clearer idea of your true goals and objectives and a solid plan for how to achieve them, we show you how to select the components of a portfolio that will allow you to attain financial success, while minimizing the risk along the way.

We also examine the client/advisor relationship, which is key to ensuring your financial success. We consider the client/advisor relationship to be a mini strategic alliance. Drawing on Maria's years of experience creating large corporate alliances, we demonstrate how the same techniques can be applied here to improve relations between you and your advisor. Additionally, we offer Mindfulness tips that will help ensure that readers can optimize communication with their advisor— including how to tell if someone is really listening, if they're not being forthcoming, or if they're withholding information.

Inevitably, things will go awry at some point; divorce, job loss, or a market meltdown can wreak havoc on an investment portfolio. Mindfulness can help to guide you through the crisis, and we show you some techniques that will help you to maintain your equanimity in times of great stress.

Finally, we take a look at the end, and plan with the end in mind. What doesn't make sense to us is that everyone has fire insurance for their house, yet many people don't have adequate life insurance. Relatively few houses burn down, but everyone is guaranteed to die—yes, even you. This chapter will guide readers through the minefield of estate planning and insurance. Using Mindfulness, we teach you to consider what you truly want to have happen and what kind of legacy is important to you. Yes, it's more goal setting, but this time for your death, as opposed to your life.

Our goal is to help you experience greater fulfillment and less suffering. The strategies in our book will help you to increase Mindfulness in every aspect of your life. Used in tandem with sound financial planning principles, Mindfulness will help you to create a secure future. You will see that by achieving clarity, staying focused, and applying equanimity, you can attain both financial success and peace of mind. It's just a matter of tuning out the noise of the world, and tuning in to your awareness.

The Authors

Maria Gonzalez, BCom, MBA

Maria is a 30-year business veteran who believes that Mindfulness transforms lives. She has been meditating regularly since 1991 and teaching meditation since 2002. She applies Mindfulness to all aspects of her life, both personally and professionally. As founder and president of Argonauta Strategic Alliances Consulting Inc., she ensures that Mindfulness is indistinguishable from her business, whether negotiating complex strategic alliances or coaching business leaders to use Mindfulness in their lives and businesses.

Maria's personal mission always has been to enable people to achieve their best by helping them help themselves. When someone is suffering from stress, they're unable to focus and make good decisions or even to enjoy life. As a founding member and Vice Chair of the Global Business and Economic Roundtable on Addictions and Mental Health, she knows the toll that stress can take on individuals, organizations, and society. She's witnessed first-hand how Mindfulness meditation can enable those who practise the techniques regularly to benefit from the ability to create calm and focus at will, and to see clearly under stressful circumstances. This enables them to make sound decisions. She sees the impact of this on their lives and their businesses every day.

Her passion is the application of Mindfulness to daily life and she has coached hundreds of people to apply it while in a meeting, making a presentation, developing corporate strategy, negotiating a deal, on an airplane, on a treadmill, or on the golf course. Maria believes that Mindfulness is completely applicable to money. We can either handle money mindfully and derive pleasure from it, or it can control us and our lives and make us miserable.

Graham Byron, CFP

Graham has been an Investment Advisor and planner for more than 20 years. During that time he has spoken at hundreds of workshops and seminars, co-authored two other books on financial planning, worked with hundreds of clients, and talked to thousands of people about financial security. His parallel interest in the path of Mindfulness was triggered over 25 years ago when he read *Zen in the Art of Archery*. Since that time he has studied many books on the topic, most notably *I Am That*. When he found Maria, he was delighted to have someone explain to him in a secular, non-threatening, and surprisingly simple way how to achieve peace, clarity, and a reduction of stress. A welcome side effect was playing the best nine holes of golf in his life.

At this turning point in our financial lives, he feels that it makes sense to share the topic of Mindfulness and its application to money. He hopes that people will use it in their financial planning process, so they will be able to maintain a state of calm awareness, make good decisions, and enjoy their wealth.

Chapter 1

How We Got Here and How We'll Get Out

For the dozen years leading up to the financial crisis of 2008, we experienced unprecedented growth, which created unrealistic expectations. We thought that the sky was the limit and the only way was up. Prosperity seemed permanent, and the old rules of cause and effect no longer applied. We believed in our entitlement instead of our responsibility to ourselves, each other, and the world. And then it all came to a screeching halt.

"Over the past two years, we have faced the most severe financial crisis since the Great Depression. The financial system failed to perform its function as a reducer and distributor of risk. Instead, it magnified risks, precipitating an economic contraction that has hurt families and businesses around the world," wrote Timothy F. Geithner, U.S. Treasury Secretary, and Lawrence Summers, Director of the National Economic Council, in a *Washington Post* commentary.[1]

Trillions of dollars disappeared from the North American economy, and financial markets dropped more than 44% from their highs. Banks went under, companies big and small declared bankruptcy, people lost their jobs and their homes.

How did it happen? The misguided behaviour of businesses, advisors, and individuals combined to create a perfect storm. As President Obama noted in a *Wall Street Journal* interview, "We had a massively overleveraged consumer, a massively overleveraged corporate sector, and a financial system that did not have much restraint."[2] Individuals became enmeshed in a vicious cycle of greed and fear. As our prosperity grew, so too did our fear that we'd somehow lose it, so we became greedy for even more.

Ironically, people began suffering even before the crisis took hold. We were seldom able to experience fulfillment because our cravings for more became insatiable. We came to believe that it was our right to have a home, a cottage, two cars, a boat, and on and on. We lost touch with our core and what we truly wanted, and focused on the illusion of what we thought we wanted—always more, more, more. We didn't take the time to stop and savour what we already had accomplished or attained. We all were seeking happiness, but became misguided as to what constitutes happiness.

Organizations fared no better. They also fell victim to the trap of continually wanting more—more profits, more revenue, more market share; maximization became king. One of the greatest strategic flaws that led us here was the maximiz-ation of shareholder value, which gained popularity over the past 15 years. Businesses came to believe that stock price was paramount, and optimizing market value took precedence over the needs of stakeholders. As public interest in investing and financial markets grew, stock analysts gained greater and greater power, and soon management teams found themselves focused more on monthly results than long-term strategies. A positive comment from an analyst meant that share prices would go up, and shareholders would be happy.

Soon enough, the situation devolved into a type of free-for-all. Management and board members were benefitting greatly from increased share prices, and their stock options were priced and in some cases repriced as the situation dictated. Generous bonuses were granted for short-term achievements. This flawed compensation strategy perpetuated unfortunate outcomes. People are smart; they quickly learn what behaviours are rewarded and follow suit so that they can benefit as well. This led to a disconnect between clients, employees, and management—anyone who wasn't a shareholder. For a long time this appeared to be the norm and institutions who didn't follow this strategy were viewed to be out of step and potentially not competitive.

Said President Obama, "I don't think I am alone in believing that the incentive structure in many companies has not been to reward high performance; that you had huge compensation packages for people who ran their companies into the ground, and that there was very little oversight from either shareholders or compensation committees on the board. We also had a situation in which, as a consequence of some of these huge incentive packages, financial firms in particular were taking some exorbitant risks to feed the short-term bottom line that weakened the system as a whole."[3]

Investment advisors weren't immune either. As clients and advisors watched the market confidently surge ahead, and recover quickly from any temporary downswings, their thinking about how they ran their lives and portfolios changed. Many fell victim to the "I don't want to be left behind" mindset. Advisors received calls and emails from normally conservative clients. The clients berated their advisors for modest returns and demanded to take more risk so they could realize more returns. Brokers in the U.S. began to face lawsuits for not generating high enough returns for their clients, a sure sign that things had gotten out of control. Advisors began to fear that if their approach was too conservative, they'd lose clients. This was unthinkable in a rising market where their colleagues seemed to be making money hand over fist. As a result, many advisors bent to client wishes and abandoned their model and skill set in order to chase the higher returns.

Even advisors who maintained their focus and stayed the course felt the effects of the downturn. They were guided by analyst reports that were based on an incomplete picture— presenting favourable short-term numbers provided by companies eager to maintain shareholder confidence—rather than a more meaningful balance, reflecting the short- and long-term perspectives.

While many are eager to place the blame on big businesses, greedy investment dealers, or unscrupulous individuals, the truth is that all parties had a hand in creating this economic crisis. For the most part we were all misguided. Individuals and organizations were greedy and fed off one another. We forgot how to be of service, and wanted rather to be served. We forgot how to be responsible, and instead became entitled. Not everyone fell into the trap, but globally enough did that there were widespread repercussions, and now we must find our way back. We are all capable of creating a better situation going forward. In fact, the crisis is deep enough that it requires a unified effort for lasting progress to be made.

THE HOUSE OF CARDS FALLS

The financial crisis of 2008 should have been predictable; after all, it had been in the making for over a decade. As individuals yearned for more material goods in their lives, seemingly at any price, institutions willingly complied by providing financing even in less than ideal situations. As the economy continued to grow, individuals were employed and at least were able to keep up the pretense of prosperity by maintaining payments on their loans, even if only the interest portion. However, when things started to fall apart and unemployment ballooned, loan payments became out of reach; cheap credit suddenly seemed very expensive. It was a symbiotic relationship—the more individuals spent, the more they were lent. In turn the lending institutions made more money, management made bigger bonuses, more stock options were issued, and everyone seemed to have more money. Until they didn't.

As we lost touch with reality, ourselves, and the world around us, we became unclear about our motives. We became ill at ease with what is, and wanted what is not. People came to fear being seen as failures—failing to accumulate as much as others as fast as others. We became slaves to stuff and it seemed we could no longer function without conditions of plenty. We became our own worst critics when the market failed to give us what we wanted.

We ran into trouble because of our attachment to endless gain, our fear of having less than others, our delusion that the prosperity could go on forever, and the fact that our pride and self-worth became intertwined with material goods. Falling prey to these hindrances made the economy a house of cards.

Soon the blame game began. When times were good we spent extravagantly and felt good about ourselves. The more we accumulated, the more our minds, and our neighbours, told us what we were worth. When it all came crashing down, we blamed others for compromising our prosperity and forcing us to wake up from the dream. The crisis seemed to shatter our very identities. Who are we without all the stuff? We essentially became controlled by our minds.

A BETTER WAY

The practice of Mindfulness can transform lives by enabling us to experience peace of mind and fulfillment in everyday life. It's scientifically proven to be effective in the management and reduction of stress, and regularly practising Mindfulness meditation actually rewires the brain for greater happiness. Don't panic, Mindfulness meditation is secular and requires no chanting or patchouli. Tiger Woods is well known for meditating to focus and stay calm, and his success is undeniable. Phil Jackson, the coach of the L.A. Lakers—and noted as the coach with the greatest number of NBA Championship titles—is also well known for his meditation practice. Many business leaders practise meditation as a way to become more effective—including Bob Shapiro, former Monsanto chief executive; William George, supervisory board member of Goldman Sachs Group Inc.; William Ford, chairman of the Ford Motor Company; and Bob Stiller, chairman of Green Mountain Coffee Roasters. Even Google Inc. began offering its staff Mindfulness meditation classes in 2007.

Since 1991 Maria has been applying Mindfulness to every aspect of her business, including developing strategy, creating joint ventures and mergers and acquisitions, and negotiating deals around the world. And as you can see in the following example, you can do it and benefit from it anytime, anywhere.

In 2006, Maria was asked to speak at a conference in Banff. After giving her presentation on the link between organizational health and financial performance, there was a question and answer period. Someone asked Maria to give an example of Mindfulness meditation, which had been one of her key recommendations for improving financial performance in organizations.

She had not intended for meditation to be part of the presentation. She thought the conditions were probably not ideal for a demonstration—500 busy business leaders and professionals being asked to sit quietly and meditate with no advance notice, at the end of a three-day conference, with flights to catch and a one-and-a-half-hour drive to the closest airport. Maria began to guide the group in a simple, 15-minute meditation. To her astonishment there was complete silence and stillness in the room for the full 15 minutes.

Afterward, Maria was mobbed by a crowd. There were so many questions and so much interest. Numerous people commented on the fact that they had rarely experienced such calmness and relaxation so quickly and wanted to introduce Mindfulness to their companies.

We believe that Mindfulness is an easily learned skill that will help you to think more clearly, make better decisions, focus on your true goals, and find success. After all, surely replacing greed and desperation with calm and focus when considering your finances greatly enhances your chances of success and happiness. As Louis Pasteur said, "Chance favours the prepared mind."

Our goals in writing this book include:

- Introducing you to ways to reduce and manage stress
- Teaching you how to bring focus, clarity, and equanimity to your life and finances

- Helping clients and advisors reach a new level of understanding between them that will improve their relations and enable both sides to listen clearly and end up as allies on the same side of the table

Maria will introduce you to the basics of Mindfulness meditation, including its history, techniques you can apply immediately in your life, and five common hindrances to success. Graham will review solid financial planning principles for you. And together we will show you how to apply Mindfulness techniques to financial planning so you can achieve greater financial success and peace of mind.

When we don't know ourselves and don't create our own strategy for our lives, by default we follow someone else's. Finding fulfillment and happiness this way isn't possible. Practising Mindfulness allows us to focus on what we really want, which is to know who and what we are. It enables you to proactively train your mind so that you can control your mind. Don't get us wrong—we value money and enjoy what it can give us. But we also value balancing the long and short term, optimization, making decisions that support a life well lived, being clear about our objectives, changing what we can change, and accepting what we can't.

Mindfulness is about being engaged and awake in the world and your life. It's about decreasing suffering and increasing fulfillment. When you are mindful, you can make money work for you, rather than being worked by your money.

Chapter 2

An Introduction to Mindfulness Meditation

Mindfulness *is simply noticing* the way things are. It's not a technique, it's a skill—the skill of being aware without grasping or denying. Both grasping and denying are created states, they don't occur naturally. Therefore, Mindfulness is the skill of being natural. It enables you to be aware of exactly where and what you are.

It's rooted in a 2,500-year-old science of the mind called Vipassana. Translated, *Vipassana* means insight meditation or Mindfulness meditation. Although the ancient science of Mindfulness meditation began in Buddhism, it can be taught and practised without religious beliefs, and is applicable to the challenges of modern-day life. Indeed, it's increasingly gaining popularity today, with such high-profile people as Tiger Woods, Phil Jackson, Oprah Winfrey, Richard Gere, Sting, Sheryl Crow, Leonard Cohen, Shania Twain, Paul McCartney, Ringo Starr, Tina Turner, Goldie Hawn, Al Gore, and Bill Ford (of Ford Motors), among many others, all praising the benefits of a meditation practice.

Mindfulness meditation trains us to be attentive and conscious about what's happening in any given moment through the use of specific techniques. It's the method or technique of intentionally becoming natural—it sounds like an oxymoron, but it works. Mindfulness meditation trains the mind to be in the present moment without distractions, and to concentrate on whatever you choose, for as long as you choose.[1]

As you use Mindfulness meditation techniques to train your mind, you gain control of it. Understand that an untrained mind tends to be controlled by thoughts and feelings, and is subject to much greater outside influence. For example, conversations, poor results in the financial markets, and the receipt of bills or financial statements can negatively impact an untrained mind much more than one that's trained to allow distractions to arise without reacting to them and that can see them for what they are. Essentially, an untrained mind can become a runaway train, taking away your inner peace, happiness, and state of well-being.

Mindfulness meditation uses specific techniques and exercises that help you deepen your ability to concentrate (we discuss these techniques in chapter 3). When you exercise your body with the proper techniques, you become stronger, more flexible, and have greater endurance. Likewise, the more you exercise your brain by meditating with the proper techniques, the more deeply you'll be able to concentrate and the greater clarity you'll achieve—about yourself and the world around you. Additionally, you'll begin to experience *equanimity*, which as mentioned in the preface refers to the ability to accept "what is arising within you" without resistance, and to accept what you can't change. With training you'll experience equanimity about the financial markets and your portfolio's performance. You'll continue to change what you can about your portfolio so that it's more in line with your goals and risk preferences, and you'll accept what you can't change, such as interest rates or foreign exchange.

The application of this ancient science of the mind in a broad way requires techniques that are accessible to our contemporary culture. Maria's teacher, Shinzen Young, has made a significant contribution with his innovative Mindfulness techniques. Like good science, the techniques are elegant and simple, but not too simple. A number of his teachings are contained and cited in this chapter, and some of the techniques are described in chapter 3.

TRAIN YOUR BRAIN

Dr. Richard Davidson, a neuroscientist, has been studying the results of meditation at the University of Wisconsin–Madison since 1992. "[Davidson's] newest results from the meditation study . . . take the concept of neuroplasticity a step further by showing that mental training through meditation . . . can in itself change the inner workings and circuitry of the brain . . . Meditation not only changes the workings of the brain in the short term, but also quite possibly produces permanent changes."[2]

Dr. Davidson's research shows that meditation results in improvements in mental activities such as focus, memory, learning, and heightened awareness, as well as positive thoughts and emotions. He has concluded that in addition to these short-term benefits, meditation training and practice may produce permanent changes in the brain. And the really good news is that modern neuroscience shows that our minds are as elastic as our bodies, and can be trained to improve at any age. Dr. Davidson says, "What we found is that the longtime practitioners [of meditation] showed brain activation on a scale we have never seen before. . . . Their mental practice is having an effect on the brain in the same way golf or tennis practice will enhance performance." It demonstrates, he says, that the brain is capable of being trained and physically modified in ways few people had imagined.[3]

KEY TERMS

Throughout this book we use four terms that are key in Mindfulness meditation:

Equanimity

Refers to the ability to accept "what is" without resistance. After all, if something's already so, what's the benefit of resisting? Equanimity refers to accepting things you can't control. You can't control the financial markets, so being equanimous is a healthy strategy. Of course, this doesn't mean you must accept everything as is and not make changes. If you're unhappy with a situation and are in a position to change it, then do so. If you can make appropriate changes to your portfolio and maintain a calm perspective, then by all means do so. We're not advocating a passive or indifferent attitude, but rather a gentle matter-of-factness with your sensory experience. Literally, equanimity means balance; in practical terms it means don't fight with yourself. It refers to an attitude of not interfering with the operation of the six senses (hearing, seeing, smelling, tasting, the feeling body, and the thinking mind)[4] or sensory experience.

Concentration

Is the ability to maintain your undivided attention on something you choose for as long as you choose. When you are mindful, you're able to allow distractions to remain in the background while you focus on the task at hand. A positive cycle arises whereby your ability to concentrate makes you feel calmer, and in turn, your calmness facilitates greater concentration. Additionally, the more you're able to concentrate, the deeper your clarity becomes. Your increasing ability to focus and concentrate will make you more effective and efficient, freeing up time and allowing you to stay on plan and to see opportunities that previously may have been obscured. This means you'll be able to stay focused on what matters. When your advisor explains aspects of your portfolio or answers your questions, you'll be able to really listen to what's being said and not be distracted by your own thoughts.

Clarity

Pertains to being clear and aware of what is going on, both internally and in the world at large. The greater your clarity the better you're able to make decisions, because you understand what drives you, including when you distract yourself because you're uncomfortable about what you become aware of or realize. Clarity about your financial priorities and your life's purpose will make it less likely that you'll become clouded by mixed feelings about your financial situation (we talk more about this in chapter 5).

Purification

Is a technical term referring to the clearing away of negative habitual patterns. We all have sources of unhappiness within us, and when you clear them away you can experience true freedom. As you observe what arises and do nothing to interfere, you experience purification. This results in dissolving the blockages to happiness—you reveal your intrinsic happiness, the nature of your consciousness, which is effortless joy.[5] Suddenly you'll start to experience true liberation and this frees up a tremendous amount of energy. This can be particularly beneficial if you've previously developed an unhealthy relationship with money.

In Mindfulness meditation, extraordinary attention is paid to ordinary experience. This attention, when applied with equanimity, produces insight and purification. The insight attained is a deep understanding about profound universal issues, such as how it is that pain turns into suffering and how it is that pleasure becomes satisfaction or neediness, and how it is that the sense of self arises.[6] When you observe what's happening, particularly internally, and don't interfere, you experience purification, which dissolves blockages to happiness. It takes a lot of energy to try to control everything and ensure that things are exactly "right." When you let go of this need to control, you'll start to experience liberation and free up energy. You'll have a sense of freedom and happiness that isn't dependent on conditions or circumstances. When you apply equanimity, you're more powerful because your actions come from a place of awareness and non-attachment—hence decisions are made based on fact rather than emotion.

During the financial meltdown in the fall of 2008, those who were trained in Mindfulness and were able to apply equanimity to their situations were less likely to make rash decisions about their portfolios; they were able to consider all of the implications before making decisions and taking action. They were able to listen to what was being said by their advisors, rather than falling prey to their fears of what might be looming in the future. Recognizing that these markets were unpredictable, they focused on what they could control rather than what they couldn't. Despite experiencing anxiety, they allowed it to fully arise in them without resistance and without catastrophizing about what might be, therefore they were able to control their minds and didn't suffer as they would have if they'd allowed their thoughts to run wild.

THE PRICE OF STRESS

Stress is so commonplace now; it just seems like a way of life. The demands of balancing family life, work, school, and some semblance of a social life while also figuring out how to pay the mortgage while saving for retirement and the kids' education leave many feeling overwhelmed. And this stress comes at a price. Over time it affects our ability to make decisions, our judgment, our relationships, and our health. To maintain well-being, it's important to develop and cultivate the "relaxation response" (a term coined at the Harvard Medical School in the 1970s by Dr. Herbert Benson)[7]. Essentially the *relaxation response* is the ability to create calm at will. With practice, Mindfulness will enable you to do just that.

Humans are equipped with a basic flight or fight instinct that dates back to caveman times. In those days it was very beneficial—your brain didn't wait around to find out if the threatening noise behind you came from a bear or a mouse; sensing danger, it told you to run. This was essential for the preservation of the species. In modern times, however, it's rarely an appropriate response. But because the human brain is still wired the same way, the flight or fight instinct still can be raised. If you're sitting in a meeting and you sense something going wrong, it's probably inappropriate to run, but unfortunately the response is still activated. Unless you're able to relax yourself and work through the adrenalin, it stays in your system as stress and negatively affects you, both physically and emotionally. The bottom line is that when you're stressed you're driven by fear or worry, your system isn't at ease, and your well-being is compromised.

With meditation practice you'll be able to create a gap between stimulus and response (a term coined by Steven Covey)[8] and, with further practice, to widen that gap. The more you practise Mindfulness, the wider that gap can become, and this makes it easier to create and maintain perspective when you're making decisions. This helps to keep stress at bay, and rather than being driven by emotion and behaving irrationally and impulsively, you'll be able to calmly and clearly assess a situation and make better decisions. At the same time, you'll lessen the physiological stress on yourself.

The following stress-related statistics are quite clear, and a sad reality of our time. And consider that these were compiled before the 2008 market collapse and economic recession. In fact, these statistics were compiled in a time of unprecedented prosperity. Just imagine how much worse they'll be going forward.

- U.S. companies lose an estimated $200 billion annually in absenteeism, subpar performance, tardiness, and workers' compensation claims related to stress.[9]

- Stress-related ailments account for more than 60% of visits made to doctors.[10]

- The cost of absenteeism, which is primarily because of stress, has increased by 50% in the last decade. Direct and indirect costs of absenteeism, including costs for replacement workers and lost productivity, account for 17% of a total payroll.[11]

BENEFITS OF MINDFULNESS MEDITATION

Interesting things happen when you practise the techniques of Mindfulness meditation. The first thing you'll experience is a greater sense of calm. You'll suddenly feel more relaxed. Over time, situations that once caused stress don't seem worth worrying about. Life seems more pleasant and fulfilling. You'll be better able to savour positive experiences and deal with difficult or painful ones. You'll have more confidence in your ability to handle life's adversities, such as illness or an economic crisis. While the difficulty will still exist, being equanimous makes it bearable. When you're equanimous you accept what is and make better decisions because you're able to keep your wits about you when others can't. Additionally, Mindfulness training dramatically increases your general concentration ability. This is critical because concentration power is the single most universally applicable and most deeply empowering skill that a human being can cultivate.

Much research has been done on the physiological effects of reducing stress, and Mindfulness meditation's role in this. Mindfulness meditation provides a host of benefits in people's lives, both personally and professionally. The following benefits are consistently reported by the people I coach and the organizations I work with, including

Personal/Health Benefits

- A brain rewired for greater focus and happiness
- Improved immune system
- Lowered blood pressure
- A healthier heart
- Improved ability to handle stress and greater calmness

Organizational/Professional Benefits

- Increased personal resilience, and the ability to sustain their performance
- Better judgment and decision making
- Improved concentration on the task at hand and an enhanced ability to stay focused, making them more effective
- An ability to prioritize

- Enhanced capacity to work on multiple projects because of their enhanced ability to focus on a single task in a given moment, thereby becoming much more effective and efficient
- Improved time management
- An ability to anticipate and serve client needs
- Creativity

When teams are trained jointly, they report:

- Improvement in team effectiveness, including more efficient and effective meetings of significantly shorter duration
- Improvement in team performance and fewer misunderstandings
- The ability to determine what underlies most conflicts and arrive at a mutually beneficial conclusion
- Greater innovation and inspiration
- An enhanced ability to anticipate and serve client needs
- Overall greater productivity at all levels of the organization

IN SUMMARY

Overall, individuals who practise Mindfulness meditation report greater satisfaction with their lives and greater personal happiness. They describe an improved ability to connect with colleagues, family, and friends. They report less stress and a significantly improved ability to sleep. A common theme is their experience of a vastly improved quality of life.

You too can experience these benefits, but success requires two conditions. The first is motivation; you need to have an interest and desire to do this training of the mind, aimed at helping yourself. The other condition is practice. In order to experience benefits, ideally you need to practise the proper techniques on a daily basis. It's possible to experience benefits with as little as 10 to 15 minutes per day. Naturally a daily investment of 20–30 minutes will bring about greater potential benefits, but the key is consistency and momentum. Better to practise for 10 minutes every day than 30 minutes twice per week.

One of the greatest immediate benefits of practising Mindfulness is the ability to gain control of your mind and thereby your life. This ability is imperative for personal and professional success. The beauty is that your baseline concentration, clarity, and equanimity, with continued practice, increases permanently.[12] As with physical exercise, the benefits that are derived from Mindfulness practice aren't only experienced during the actual practice, but throughout the entire day. In fact, you'll often become aware of how much your life has changed when an experience that previously would have seemed devastating is experienced as merely inconvenient or unfortunate. A market crash can be experienced as disruptive and unfortunate, rather than devastating. This is in marked contrast to those who in history have taken their own lives because they saw themselves as financially ruined.

The key message is simple—you can use the power of your mind to regain control of your mind. This enables you to create optimal effectiveness in your personal and professional life. Mindfulness meditation becomes beneficial to your mental and physical health, to your happiness, to the prosperity of your organizations, and indeed to society as a whole. Essentially, Mindfulness meditation has the potential to transform lives.

Still unsure about how something so seemingly simple can be so powerful? Check out the research section below for some amazing findings.

The Research

Below is a small sampling of the abundant scientific research that has been conducted into the effectiveness of meditation, and the conclusions drawn by the scientific community.

- Men with coronary artery disease were able to improve their heart rate, blood pressure, and work performance by meditating 20 minutes twice daily for six to eight months.[13]

- Cardiologist Dr. John Zamarra states, "there is more research on the benefits of meditation than any other medical procedure to improve health. It has been found that hospital admissions for cardiovascular disease were

reduced by an astounding 87% among long-term meditators. The research was well controlled; these patients still
had routine medical exams and physicals, so there was no
confounding reason that they might have been merely
avoiding medical care. If there was a cardiovascular drug
that even approached 87% effectiveness, it would be considered a miracle drug."[14]

- Research has found Mindfulness meditation to be very
effective in the prevention of depression and its treat-
ment. Researchers have found a 44% reduction in the risk
of relapse in those with two or more depressions, a group
that is typically challenging to treat.[15]

- According to the Center for Creative Leadership, the
average worker is interrupted every 11 minutes. Even
more interesting is that it takes these same workers about
25 minutes to get back to the original task.[16] The issue of
lost productivity is huge. No wonder we can end our day
and feel like we have been very busy yet not have accomplished a great deal. With Mindfulness training, no matter
how often you're interrupted, it only takes seconds to
return to your original task. This means individuals who
have a trained mind are able to accomplish a great deal in
short periods of time, without frustration at having been
interrupted. Additionally, tasks don't need to be done
more than once, making you more efficient and able to
accomplish much more in a single period of time.

- "For decades, researchers at the National Institutes of Health, the University of Massachusetts, and the Mind/Body Medical Institute at Harvard University have sought to document how meditation enhances the qualities companies need in their human capital: sharpened intuition, steely concentration, and plummeting stress levels. What's different today is groundbreaking research showing that when people meditate, they alter the biochemistry of their brains. The evolution of powerful mind-monitoring technologies such as MRIs and EEGs has also enabled scientists to scan the minds of meditators on a microscopic scale, revealing fascinating insights about the plasticity of the mind and meditation's ability to sculpt it."[17]

- Dr. Jon Kabat-Zinn has done extensive research into the health benefits of Mindfulness meditation, and he and Dr. Richard Davidson collaborated "on a recent study of workers in a high-tech company who took a two-month training program in meditation. It showed significant changes in brain activity, declines in anxiety, and beneficial changes in immune function."[18]

- In two companies that introduced meditation, managers and employees who regularly practised meditation also reported significant reductions in health problems such as headaches and backaches, improved quality of sleep, and a significant reduction in the use of hard liquor and cigarettes, compared to personnel in the control groups.[19]

- According to Dr. Herbert Benson, "If businesses were clever, what they would do is simply put time aside [and have] a quiet room for people to carry out a meditative behavior of their choice."[20]

- Maria Gonzalez, as vice chair and a founding member of the Global Business and Economic Roundtable on Addictions and Mental Health, states, "It has become clear to me that in order to create and sustain 'healthy organizations' it is imperative that the mental health of individuals at all levels of the organization be a priority. Our research on Healthy Organizations suggests that individuals experiencing undue stress are not able to perform optimally, thereby representing an opportunity cost in terms of organizational performance, significant corporate health care costs, and a significant cost to society at large."[21] In a *Globe and Mail* interview, she said, "As business leaders, one of our key interests is sustainable performance. There can be no sustainable performance without organizational health."[22]

You can clearly see that Mindfulness works wonders on health and performance. When applied to your finances, it has similar potential to transform the way you approach investing and your relationship with money.

Chapter 3

Mindfulness Techniques

As previously mentioned, it's possible for you to gain control of your mind by training it. Training your mind enables you to experience greater calm, have more peace of mind, make better decisions, discover what truly matters to you, and find fulfillment in your life. In this chapter we'll describe some generic Mindfulness techniques that can be applied both to financial planning and to life in general. In later chapters, we'll introduce you to some techniques that can be particularly helpful with the various aspects of financial planning, including developing a strong relationship with your advisor.

The goal is, over time, to begin living mindfully throughout the day. In order to achieve this, you need to start by meditating regularly and developing a daily (or almost daily) practice. This will cause you to experience greater calm and to develop focus or concentration in your life. The spillover benefits from adding formal sitting practice into your daily life will occur naturally. But, in order to leverage the benefits of your formal practice and maximize their potential, you must also employ Mindfulness strategies in action. These are specific strategies that you can use anytime—while walking the dog, driving, playing golf, sitting in a meeting, developing your financial objectives, reading the stock ticker, buying a business, selling a business—you get the picture. Mindfulness is applicable to everything that occurs during your day, whether personal or professional. My coaching experience has shown me that the students who pay special attention to using Mindfulness in their daily lives greatly accelerate their ability to develop the skill of Mindfulness. By applying these strategies consistently, they're being proactive and, in time, they start to be mindful without conscious effort.

With this in mind, throughout the chapter I'll introduce you to techniques for both formal practice and strategies for Mindfulness in action. Don't panic and think you'll never be able to do this; we have never worked with anyone who was motivated to learn and who practised regularly (as little as 10 minutes per day) who couldn't do this and experience the benefits.

When dealing with money, as with almost all other aspects of life, the five most important things are

1. The ability to calm yourself in the face of stress or difficult decisions

2. The ability to understand what's going on within yourself and how you perceive your reality; to understand what drives you and how you think and feel about what arises

3. The ability to be in the present moment and clearly understand what you're hearing or reading and not be

caught up in regretting or reliving the past or fearing and catastrophizing the future

4. To imagine and create in your mind a life that is positive and fulfilling, and to set in motion positive outcomes in your life

5. And finally, to know that all things come to pass and that nothing is forever, whether it's good or bad. This applies equally to bull markets and to market collapses

Please note: Audio recordings of guided meditations featuring the various techniques described in this chapter are available at www.themindfulinvestor.com and www.argonautaconsulting.com. You may find these particularly helpful when you first begin your practice.

RELAXATION TECHNIQUES

You can do these techniques sitting up in a chair or lying down. Try the techniques in both positions to see which helps you reach maximum relaxation.

The Breath

It's not uncommon for us to tell someone who's visibly stressed to "take a breath," and there are sound reasons for this. Typically when we're stressed our breath becomes more shallow or uneven, which creates a cycle that causes even greater stress. By taking a conscious breath you can slow things down.

Make it a slow, even breath. You might try breathing in for a count of three or four and out for a count of three or four. Doing this for five minutes or so will relax you greatly. Be sure to pay attention only to the breath and count as you are inhaling and exhaling. When you become distracted by your own thoughts that might say, "this won't help one bit," or "I hope this helps, but what if it doesn't," et cetera, very gently bring your thoughts back to the breath. At first you may need to bring yourself back dozens of times in a five-minute period, but don't despair—distraction is perfectly normal.

Concentrating on your breathing is also a good strategy in daily life and can help to calm you as you're about to open your bills or financial statements or make an unpleasant phone call. You may not need to breathe for the full five minutes in these circumstances; just stopping to take one or two breaths may suffice to remind you to be mindful, to be in the present moment and not to be hijacked by your runaway thoughts.

Think of the breath as your ally. It's an internal relaxation mechanism available to you 24 hours a day. You can consciously access it any time you want to gain perspective or widen the gap between stimulus and response so that you can make better decisions.

Body Relaxation

Another technique is to systematically relax your body. Begin with your feet. Relax them, and let go of any tension. Then move your way up the body to the lower leg, then the upper leg, and continue to work your way up to the trunk, the back, the shoulders and arms, the neck, and the head. As you're doing this, focus only on relaxing the body part you are working with and maintaining relaxation in the parts you have already worked with. As with the breath technique, if your mind wanders or becomes critical, very gently bring it back into focus without judging yourself. When you have relaxed your whole body to the best of your ability, try to remain relaxed for a few minutes. At this point your focus of concentration is the whole body and the enjoyment of being relaxed.

As you gain experience, you'll be able to relax your whole body in as little as five minutes, and eventually in seconds. If you use this as a daily formal practice, you can do it in 10–30 minutes depending on your available time.

Strategies for Mindfulness in Action

In daily life you can use awareness as a strategy to calm your body at will. Train yourself to tune in to your body periodically during the day and see whether you are holding tension anywhere. If you're like most people, you may have a particular part of the body that tightens under stress. Commonly this is the shoulders, the neck, the stomach, or the back, but it could be any other part of the body. By tuning in periodically, you become more familiar with your own body as well as with situations that cause you stress.

For the first week, merely tune in to the body throughout the day and pay attention to what you discover. Are you tense or relaxed? Is there a part(s) of the body that is (are) often tense? Under what circumstances do you become tense? Simply become aware; change nothing. You may find that just by placing awareness on the tense area you become more relaxed. In other cases, you may actually realize how tense you are and not become relaxed at all. This is fine; all you're looking for during this first week is awareness.

After the first week, every time you tune in to the body and find a tense area, purposefully relax it to the best of your ability. Notice that I am saying, "to the best of your ability." At first some people find their ability to relax systematically is very modest, but don't be concerned—it's not a problem. With persistence it will improve, so be prepared to amaze yourself. Also, note that every day is a different day, every moment a different moment. One day you may not be able to relax very much while the next day you can loosen everything and vice versa. Be patient and don't become discouraged.

The following formal techniques of Internal Awareness, External Awareness, and Creating/Imagining Positive Outcomes were developed by Shinzen Young.

INTERNAL AWARENESS

Life is lived in the mind. Perception is reality to us. Sometimes we seem to be stuck in our heads, so to speak. We relive the past, trying to correct a situation that we think we could have handled better. We worry about what might happen in the future: if our investments drop in value, if inflation goes up, if the kids don't get a job, if we lose a job, and on and on. For the most part, the worry and fear involve things that will never happen, and we all know that reliving the past won't change any of it, so why focus on either? Most of our mind space is spent in the past or the future, but with a trained mind you can spend more time in the present moment, which is where life is lived. Remember that the mind is a trickster and not always reliable. You can't believe every thought or every feeling you have.

We all think in mental images and/or in mental talk that arises in the form of hearing ourselves carry on conversations in our heads. We can also hear the voices of others in our heads, as when we play back a conversation that may have happened earlier in the day. This is known as *the thinking mind*. In terms of the thinking process, in some cases there's only talk or only images, yet in other cases the thinking mind may manifest as both images and talk.

You can also experience *the feeling body*, which refers to sensations in the body that are associated with emotion. These may result from an image or mental talk, and can be pleasant or unpleasant. In some instances Feel sensations in the body may arise independent of the thinking mind, as with our primitive reaction of fear in the dark or, for some, fear of thunder. These sensations can occur anywhere in the body and be very subtle or very strong and evident. Examples of the feeling body include tightness in your stomach when you're anxious, tightness in the throat when you can't say what you wish to say, the expanded sensation in your chest when you're joyful, or your mouth curving up when you smile.

Together the thinking mind and the feeling body create a powerful combination. Marketers know this and use it to great benefit; they know that if they can motivate the feeling body they can get consumers to act in their favour. Often they'll show an evocative image to try and stimulate the feeling body because it's the greatest driver of behaviour. This is often done by appealing to one or more of the hindrances (see chapter 4 for more information on the five hindrances to success). Many thoughts, especially those that are emotionally charged or have a powerful grip on us, are experienced in the body. If you're not aware of the connection in the body, you can easily become hijacked by your thoughts and lose touch with the present moment, and often with what matters. This can cause you to make poor decisions and experience increasing stress.

Here's an example of this powerful combination of the thinking mind and feeling body. Imagine recounting to yourself a conversation you've just had with your financial advisor. This was a pleasant conversation with good news about your portfolio. As a result, your mind's eye has an image of the meeting or the setting where it took place. You remember the words she used to tell you that your investments have risen by 20%. Along with the image and the talk, you have a pleasant sensation in your chest or throughout the body.

Now imagine the opposite. You have just had a meeting with your advisor and she tells you that your portfolio has declined by 40%. You leave her office and drive home, but you don't remember any of the drive. Who knows how you got home. Throughout the entire ride you saw the image of the office and the advisor. Over and over again you hear the advisor say that now you have 40% less than you did. Your stomach is in knots, your hands are clammy, and you are starting to get a tension headache. Now new images arise, images of losing your home, of the conversation you will have with your family. You imagine being poor (at least poorer than you were). This brings about deeper sensations in the body. Now you experience nausea, your blood pressure rises, your heart rate rises, your face is flushed.

This is a clear example of the thinking mind and the feeling body reinforcing one another and escalating sensations, potentially to a state of panic. This wasn't an unusual reaction as the market plunged into turmoil toward the end of 2008. You can well imagine how health becomes compromised and judgment becomes impaired in these moments. The person in this example went from hearing an unpleasant fact—a 40% drop in the portfolio—to catastrophizing that they would be homeless and destitute. Now, we're not minimizing the significance of these losses; they're serious and unpleasant. But in this present moment, nothing has changed.

It's critical that you understand that the feeling body can drive behaviour, which can seriously impair judgment. Imagine the person in the example stays awake all night worrying, gripped by the fear of what will happen in the future. By morning he has decided to sell his entire portfolio before it's "too late." He calls his advisor with the instruction to sell and his advisor can't convince him to hold off. While this may be the right thing to do, most likely it is not; impulsive decisions often are not wise. The fear in his body simply is so great that it drives him to act impulsively.

A trained mind generally will catch itself. If the person in the example was familiar with Mindfulness techniques, he might have connected to his breath, slowed things down, and created some calm. He might have taken a few minutes to relax his body, which would have been quite tense. He would also have been aware of what his thinking mind and feeling body were experiencing, and not been hijacked by it. The technique of Internal Awareness enables you to divide and conquer what's arising so that you don't become overwhelmed. Over time you'll realize that the feeling body and the thinking mind arise and you can untangle them, preventing them from escalating and spiralling out of control.

In fact, in time and with practice, some of these techniques would kick in automatically. The person would be able to stay focused on the task at hand or the technique he chose to follow. He would be clear about what was arising within him, and able to apply equanimity to what he was experiencing. He wouldn't be fighting himself. His mind would be calm and sharp so that sound decisions would follow, and physiologically his system wouldn't be compromised. The "relaxation response" introduced in chapter 2 would kick in.

Pain and Suffering

Another key point to consider is the distinction between pain and suffering. Pain refers to the difficulties, physical or emotional, that arise in life. Pain is inevitable. This isn't a pessimistic view, it's just the reality of life. Suffering, on the other hand, is optional. Suffering occurs when you resist and aren't equanimous with whatever is arising in your sensory experience. As we mentioned in chapter 2, equanimity refers to an attitude of not interfering with the operation of the six senses (hearing, seeing, smelling, tasting, physical touch, the feeling body, and the thinking mind). When you resist, not only do you suffer, but you also perpetuate the suffering. The reality is that what you resist persists. Resisting what arises internally causes concentration, clarity, and equanimity to decrease, and as they decrease, suffering increases. According to Shinzen Young, "pain is one thing and resistance to the pain is something else, and when the two come together you have an experience of suffering . . . suffering equals pain multiplied by resistance."[1]

In the previous example, the pain was the fact that this investor's portfolio had decreased by 40%. This is an undeniable fact. The suffering refers to the catastrophizing and worrying about the future. The individual was dealing with both the portfolio loss and the extreme worry. He resisted admitting that the portfolio had dropped dramatically and that he was overwhelmed by fear. He lost his focus and equanimity, and the moment lacked clarity. The more he resisted and interfered with what was arising within him, the more his suffering increased. He was much more likely to make an impulsive decision in this state. However, if he had been trained in Mindfulness, he would still have experienced the pain of the portfolio's decline, but he wouldn't have suffered. He would have allowed himself to experience the pain fully instead of trying to distract himself from it with a drink or a piece of cake. By experiencing the pain fully he prevents suffering, because suffering = resistance × pain. When there's no resistance, there's no suffering.[2] You can see how quickly you can become overwhelmed by any situation if you're not mindful. Over time this kind of stress can take a serious toll on health and judgment, and, as a consequence, on personal and professional effectiveness.

Formal Technique

You can practise the technique of Internal Awareness (we refer to it as Feel, Image, and Talk) either sitting up in formal meditation posture or lying down.

Feel space: To start, place awareness on the parts of your body where you know you typically experience physical sensations that are associated with emotion. (This might include your stomach, where you hold tension, or your mouth, where you smile or laugh with joy.) Feel can be pleasant or unpleasant, such as a spontaneous smile or a nervous stomach. You may find that at times you experience these sensations throughout your body, as when you're so filled with fear or joy that you experience it from head to toe.

Image space: Now, also place awareness on the mental screen where you typically perceive images when your eyes are closed. This is usually in front of or behind your closed eyes.

Talk space: Finally, place awareness at your ears or around your head, wherever you typically hear the sound of your own voice or mental conversation.

Start noticing what's arising in all three of these spaces. Pay attention to one thing at a time. You may find you're primarily aware of the feeling body or of one of the two components of the thinking mind (Image or Talk), or you may even experience all three at the same time. The key is to give attention to only one at a time, even if they all arise at the same time. Do this at a leisurely pace, and find your rhythm. For example, you may notice a tight stomach; stay focused there for a few seconds. Then notice what else has come into your awareness— it may be an image of your cottage. Stay focused there for a few seconds. Then see what else has come into your awareness. It might even be the sound of your voice saying, "I feel really strange doing this."

It's entirely possible that in a given moment you're not aware of anything in your Feel, Image, or Talk spaces. This means that the three spaces are *at rest*, meaning not active. At any given time any of the spaces can be active or restful. *All rest* applies only if all three spaces are at rest at the same time; otherwise, draw your attention to an active space.

Do this for at least 10 minutes at a time. With Mindfulness technique you pay extraordinary attention to ordinary experience. The more familiar you become with your thinking mind and feeling body, the less likely you are to be hijacked by stress or impulsiveness. In using this technique the goal is not to experience total calm, but rather to notice what is arising within you at any given moment. Just notice and don't interfere. Surrender to what arises. This is the equanimity we spoke about in the previous chapter.

Three things matter when you perform this or any technique:

1. Concentration, which means that you stay focused on what you are working with

2. Clarity, which means that you know exactly what space you are noticing

3. Equanimity, which means that you accept whatever is arising internally with a gentle matter-of-factness

Strategies for Mindfulness in Action

At first you may not think of checking in with yourself during the day, so to start, tune in to the three spaces (Feel, Image, and Talk) when you experience any highly pleasant or unpleasant experience. This will make you familiar with where you experience them in your body. If you're listening to a beautiful musical performance and enjoying it thoroughly, notice what's going on internally for you in these subjective spaces. If you've just found out that your favourite stock dipped significantly, tune in to your body and see what's going on.

Doing this will train you to be self-aware and prevent you from being hijacked without realizing it. Sometimes if you're unaware, you can have an unpleasant experience in the morning and carry that with you for the rest of the day without realizing it; your mother might have called it "waking up on the wrong side of the bed." Train yourself to experience things fully as they happen, so that you don't carry them around all day long. When you have a complete experience and apply equanimity moment by moment, life appears bearable and manageable, even under significant stress.

There are many opportunities to use this technique throughout the day. For instance, become aware of what happens when you're having a difficult conversation. Is your Feel space activated? Notice this and stay with it, don't distract yourself. In a meeting, is there a conversation going on in your head while others are speaking? If there is, you'll likely have missed what was said. Have you ever noticed how many times people ask you to repeat what you just said, respond to something you never asked about, or change lanes without looking in their blind spot? All are clear signs that they were caught up in an internal story and not really present. By noticing what's going on internally when you're with others, or driving, or eating a meal, you'll become aware of how often you are in the present moment versus in your head, thinking about the past or future. As John Lennon said, "Life is what happens to you while you're busy making other plans."

EXTERNAL AWARENESS

Being aware of what's going on around you also helps to train you to live in the present moment. Why is this important? Quite simply, it's only in the present moment that anything happens; everything else is either history or fantasy. It's the best way to enjoy a sunset, the company of your family, a golf game, a ski run, a business success, et cetera. Additionally, being in the present moment allows you to make clearer decisions, have better judgment, decrease your suffering, and experience greater fulfillment in life. Living in the present moment allows you to really hear what someone says when they speak, rather than what you wish they have said or what you fear they have said. This technique will be especially useful in your conversations with your financial advisor, and in chapter 8 I'll describe in greater detail how to apply this technique. External awareness is more of an objective experience. If you're participating in a meeting with someone else who's being mindful, the likelihood is that you'll both see and hear very similar things.

Have you ever noticed how difficult it is to be in the present moment? Try looking at the palm of your hand and doing nothing else. Don't think about the hand, don't judge what you're doing, just focus on the hand. How long did you last before you became distracted? If you're like most people, it was probably only a few seconds. Why is this so hard? It's hard because an untrained mind experiences monkey mind. A *monkey mind* swings from one thing to another and back again, relentlessly. In our culture, we've turned this inability to concentrate into an erroneous interpretation of something positive, and called it multi-tasking. Multi-tasking is just an excuse that legitimizes our inability to concentrate. It's so ingrained in our culture that we've parlayed it into a desirable skill, but this couldn't be more mistaken and misguided.

In chapter 2 we mentioned a significant study that indicates that the average worker is interrupted every 11 minutes and it takes this same worker, on average, 25 minutes to get back to the original task. With training, your ability to function in the present moment will enable you to refocus within seconds. Think of how effective and efficient workers would be if they all had this ability. A 2007 *New York Times* article by Steve Lohr reported, "The human brain, with its hundred billion neurons and hundreds of trillions of synaptic connections, is a cognitive powerhouse in many ways. 'But a core limitation is an inability to concentrate on two things at once,' said René Marois, a neuroscientist and director of the Human Information Processing Laboratory at Vanderbilt University."[3] The implications are simple and clear. Even if you're doing three things at the same time, only one thing can receive your attention in any given moment. This means that if you're checking your BlackBerry and participating in a meeting, one activity is being shortchanged. If you're driving and talking or texting on your cell phone, the likelihood of an accident is greatly increased. Evidence of this is so conclusive that many major cities have banned drivers from using hand-held phones while at the wheel. A recent U.S. study published in July 2009 by the Virginia Tech Transportation Institute found that "[the] risk of being involved in [a] safety-critical event—or risk of collision—was 23.2 times greater when [drivers] were texting than when they were not distracted."[4]

The reality is that the more you multi-task, the less you're able to concentrate. Even if you're not interrupted by others, you'll begin to interrupt yourself. You may be thinking that you're far too busy to have the luxury of working on one project at a time or doing only one thing at a time. Remember that you can work on multiple projects without a problem, but only one in any given moment. By the end of the day you may have worked on four or five projects, giving each one your undivided attention when you're working on it. This makes you more efficient and effective. You'll make fewer errors and gain greater satisfaction because you'll feel like you've actually accomplished something.

Formal Technique

The concept in the following technique was popularized by Eckhart Tolle in his books *The Power of Now* and *A New Earth*, and will train you to be in the present moment. As with the technique of Internal Awareness, External Awareness encompasses three distinct spaces—Touch, Sight, and Sound.

Touch space refers to your physical body and the sensations you experience. These sensations are not associated with emotion as was the case in Feel. Instead, Touch refers to the sensation of the contact of your feet to the floor, of your clothing on your skin, of the breeze on your face. The body exists only in the present; it has no choice. Your body right now doesn't feel like it did a year ago, 10 years ago, or even 10 minutes ago. Nor does it feel the way it will tonight or next year. On the other hand, your mind does have a choice. It can live in the past, the future, and if trained, in the present moment.

Sight space refers to what you see when your eyes are open. It too exists only in the present moment. As any artist knows, the light changes throughout the day, creating different quality, shadows, et cetera.

Sound space refers to what you hear in the outside world. This too only occurs in the present moment. The airplane that just went by is gone, the presentation you're listening to is only in the present. What the presenter said 10 minutes ago is gone; even if you ask him to repeat the exact same thing it'll be a new sound—the old one is gone.

Just like with internal awareness, it's entirely possible that in a given moment you won't be aware of one of the three spaces, because it's at rest. Remember that *all rest* applies only if all three spaces are at rest; otherwise, focus your attention on an active state.

This is a wonderful technique to work with in formal practice and in daily life. As a formal practice, sit in a chair or lie on the floor in a comfortable position and place awareness on your body; this is your Touch space. Now, also place awareness on something you will softly gaze at. It can be a bowl in the centre of a table, a tree outside your window, or anything you choose; this is your Sight space. Be sure to continue to blink normally and to look at the entire object. Don't fixate on one particular part as this may strain your eyes. Finally, place awareness on the sounds around you in the room, outside the room, and outside the building; this is your Sound space.

Notice what comes into your awareness. You may become aware of one thing at a time or many things at once. Pick one to notice at a time. As with the previous technique, notice what you become aware of, focus on it for a few seconds, and then move on to either notice the same thing again, if it's still there, or something different if it's not. For example, you may become aware of your feet touching the floor. Notice that, stay focused on it for a few seconds, and then become aware of what you're noticing now. It may be your feet again, or this time it may be the sound of voices outside the room you're in. Stay focused on the sound of the voices, not the content of what's said. After focusing for a few seconds, become aware again. This time you may become aware of the tree outside your window. Pay attention to Sight for a few seconds, and continue the cycle. Find a comfortable rhythm and don't strain, just focus on what arises naturally. This will increase your concentration and create calmness. At first it may feel awkward, but keep at it and it will soon be quite pleasant and relaxing. Do this for at least 10 minutes at a time.

Strategies for Mindfulness in Action

In daily life you will find that focusing on the present moment brings great fulfillment. Connect to your feet as you walk and you'll find you are quickly in touch with your body. Look at the sights and you'll find that you discover things you have never seen before, even on routes you have taken for years. Listen to the birds sing or go to a concert and truly listen to the music—it will sound magical. Listen to what's being said and you will be amazed at what you pick up. You'll find more about this in chapter 8 as we discuss you meeting with your advisor.

This technique can be used to great advantage in every aspect of business. I have used it successfully for years when negotiating strategic alliances. It enables you to have a keen awareness of leverage points and to determine how to relate to those people across the negotiating table. It can also be used very effectively in sports. When you play any sport, connect with the body, the sights, and the sounds. If you're a runner, become aware of how your body moves as you run, and what you hear and see. If you play golf, be aware of your body as you address the ball, then just be present and swing. This is part of a more elaborate instruction, but you get the idea.

The task is simple: when you walk, walk, when you drive, drive, when you speak with someone, do nothing but listen, when you eat, just eat, when you watch a sunset, just watch the sunset. Be fully present with whatever you are doing.

You might be thinking "That sounds fine, but this leaves no room for planning or dealing with the future because it's not in the present." Of course the answer to this is that you certainly can plan for the future in the present. All that matters is that when you're planning, that's all you're doing. Planning is conscious thinking, which is very useful and necessary.

CREATING/IMAGINING POSITIVE OUTCOMES

Imagining positive things is very empowering. This is one of the reasons so many people enjoy daydreaming. We get to make up the fantasy and create the ending. Some of you may be surprised that there is a Mindfulness technique where we do precisely this. It's a form of structured daydreaming we call "Creating or Imagining Positive Outcomes."

If you play competitive sports, you may recognize this as visualizing your perfect performance. Athletes have long experienced the benefit of training the body and the mind so they both function at peak performance. Tiger Woods has become known for the ability to master the mind during competition, and he attributes this ability to meditation. Phil Jackson, the NBA coach with the greatest number of NBA Championship titles, meditates before every game. Both

Christopher Higgins and Mike Komisarek, formerly of the Montreal Canadiens hockey team, and now of the New York Rangers and Toronto Maple Leafs, respectively, use meditation as part of their training.

My experience with coaching athletes is that Mindfulness is very effective as a way of creating calm and focus at will, as well as for visualizing their best performance. This is a powerful skill that can be translated into any aspect of life, whether training for a golf match, running a race, or giving a presentation. This can also be a useful technique when developing your financial plan and creating what you want for your financial future. More about this in chapter 6.

Formal Technique

This technique involves the same spaces that were introduced in the Internal Awareness section. In that section, you worked with Feel, Image, and Talk spaces without manipulating whatever arose; however, here you're going to use the same spaces, but this time also *create* Feel, Image, and Talk.

Start by creating an image or images in the mental screen in front of or behind your eyes. For example, you can visualize yourself as being calm and relaxed. Then create your own internal talk that supports the image. You might say to yourself, "I am calm," and allow yourself to repeat this over and over again at a leisurely pace. You may find that after a while you actually experience some pleasant sensations or Pleasant

Feel in the body. If that is the case, by all means encourage it to grow. Do this for at least 10 minutes, either while seated or lying down.

This technique generates confidence and can be very powerful in creating positive outcomes. It's also good for developing concentration.

Strategies for Mindfulness in Action

You can use this technique in daily life to help create your intentions, which can be powerful things. Always intend or visualize the positive; don't create negative self talk. When you get up in the morning, you may wish to create an intention for the day. Think about what you would like to have happen. Before a meeting, spend a few minutes thinking about what your objectives are for the meeting.

There is a lot of truth to the quote by Napoleon Hill: "Whatever the mind of man can conceive and believe, it can achieve." The mind has a way of completing what we think about; just ask any golfer who has said to himself, "Don't go in the water" or "Don't go in the sand." What do you think usually happens? More often than not, they land in the water or the sand. Before meeting with your advisor, intend to have a positive and productive meeting. If you're concerned about your investments during a particular quarter, imagine being calm and equanimous as you open your financial statement, regardless of the information it contains, and then open the envelope.

Train yourself to expect the best by imagining the best. And when you catch yourself in negative self talk, take the time to notice it and create positive self talk in its place.

CONSTANT CHANGE

Nothing stays the same, we all know that. Thoughts change, feelings change, bodies change; in fact, change occurs moment by moment. Sometimes your investments do well, sometimes they don't. Sometimes whatever you touch turns to gold, sometimes you can do no right. You win some, you lose some. It's just a fact of life. But whether something is positive or negative, one thing is for sure—it will pass. In fact, it's passing moment by moment. Knowing this and keeping it in perspective can help you to get over market collapses, disappointments, and family crises. It can also help to keep expectations realistic, such as remembering that a bull market can't go on forever.

Strategies for Mindfulness in Action

When things seem like they can't get worse, proactively speak to yourself about maintaining the perspective that all things are in a constant state of change. When your stock looks like it can continue only to go up at a record rate, maintain perspective, and remember that this too will end. This may seem like a philosophical view but it's a fact. This strategy in daily life is about maintaining perspective and enabling equanimity.

You may also wish to pay attention to how much changes around you moment by moment. Notice how your thoughts change (Image space and Talk space), sometimes so much so that you can barely keep up. Note how you experience different sensations in the body (both in Touch and Feel space). Listen to how the sounds change around you—singing birds at one moment, traffic the next, construction after that, et cetera. As you drive by or walk, notice how the sights change. It all changes, nothing stays the same.

Typically we have the illusion that things stay the same because we play them back in our subjective spaces (Feel, Image, Talk), but the reality is that very often the herd has moved (so to speak) and we haven't even noticed because we're locked in our minds. The memories you relive in your mind are constantly activating the Feel space, which creates a mental loop and keeps you from being in the present moment.

NOT KNOWING/DON'T KNOW

The tendency for people is to want to know, to have answers to everything. We seek closure because that makes us comfortable. We see this in our need to make the markets certain—we want to know if the market will go up or down, or if the stock we want to buy has hit its low, and so on. But no one can know this; in fact, if you really think about it, you'll see how little we actually control or know for certain. The drive to know and to have answers to everything is simply the result of a desire for control and our discomfort with not knowing.

Part of Mindfulness is to become comfortable with Not Knowing (also known as Don't Know)—you need to practise becoming comfortable with a mind that doesn't have all the answers. This will help you to widen the gap between stimulus and response, and you'll find that in that gap many answers will surface. There are many things in life that you can readily find answers for if you don't know them; that's what Google and Wikipedia are for. What I'm referring to is different. For example, you may be deciding whether to stay with your present advisor or to look for a new one, or you may be coming to terms with your ability to handle risk. Sometimes the answer isn't immediately obvious, and you truly don't know. In these instances it may be best to allow yourself to "not know" for a period of time rather than forcing a decision because you can't bear not coming to a conclusion. See appendix A for information on how to incorporate this into your decision-making process.

Strategies for Mindfulness in Action

How many times in your day do you not know the answer to something and how does your mind react? Does it become desperate and try to grasp at some premature solution or response? This could occur anytime—when you're having conversations, in meetings, or deciding on a stock to buy. For a day or two, just notice when this happens and do nothing about it. Simply observe yourself. Then after a few days, when you have gotten into a rhythm of recognizing this in yourself, resist the temptation to find an immediate answer or premature closure. In the moment try to not resist the "Not Knowing," be equanimous with it and accept this confused state. Simply say to yourself, "I don't know," and be alright with it. Soon you'll notice that by allowing that gap to exist and to widen, answers are likely to arise more readily and your judgment will be more likely to improve.

The techniques I have described in this chapter are intended to form part of a regular, and preferably daily, practice and routine. Just 10 minutes per day has the potential to transform your life and make you a healthier, happier, and more effective person. If you are interested in working with a Mindfulness teacher, you may wish to give consideration to the points outlined in appendix C. Please be sure to take advantage of the audio recordings of guided meditations available at www.themindfulinvestor.com and www.argonautaconsulting.com to guide you as you begin your meditation practice. I also encourage you to use the strategies for Mindfulness in action so that you can experience even greater benefits. By doing both of these you will experience greater Mindfulness throughout the day in all aspects of your life. In time, you'll experience better control of your mind, so that your mind serves you and you gain more control of your life. This will enable you to maintain healthy and fulfilling relationships, including with your money, so that they can serve you well and bring you pleasure.

Chapter 4

The Five Hindrances that Impede Success

Hindrances *are mental states* that impede success. They get in the way of you realizing your full potential and experiencing fulfillment, and they cause great suffering. There are numerous hindrances, but the five most applicable to our topic are

1. Attachment

2. Aversion

3. Ignorance, confusion, and delusion

4. Envy and jealousy

5. Pride

In the descriptions below you'll see how these get in the way of making good decisions, exhibiting good judgment with your money, and experiencing fulfillment in your life.

It's important not to judge yourself negatively if you recognize that you're experiencing, or have experienced, any (or all) of these hindrances. They're simply part of being human. Everyone experiences them in some form or other during their life. Sometimes all the hindrances may be evident at the same time, and at other times you'll be aware of only one or two.

They ebb and flow and can be very intense or barely perceptible. Keep in mind that they're only problematic when they manifest in a dysfunctional way in your life. If they begin to drive your behaviour and cloud your focus, clarity, and equanimity (or acceptance of what's arising in your sensory experience—Feel/Image/Talk), then you may need to address them and re-examine your priorities (more on how to do this later in the chapter).

THE HINDRANCES

Attachment

Attachment refers to the unrelenting drive to acquire and the inability to let go. This can apply to material goods, position, status, and even beliefs. Attachment is a fixation; you become convinced that you're absolutely correct in your views and desires, no matter what they are, and then you set out to create conditions that will support these views.

This explains, in part, how so many people acquired houses that were beyond their means, and yet they still didn't consider scaling back or modifying their lifestyle when they found that they couldn't pay the mortgage. Attachment causes the house itself to become a part of their identity. Without it, their view of themselves becomes unacceptable, as if the house makes them worthy and enhances their self-esteem and position in the world.

It also explains how you can become fixated on the idea that everyone else's investments are doing better than yours. You can become attached to the idea that, somewhere, there's a silver bullet, and if only you had a better advisor or a better choice of stocks, your wealth would far exceed what it currently is.

Aversion

Aversion is the fear of losing what you have, including material goods, financial resources, social position and status, and even an argument. You become so fearful of loss that you make poor decisions. When you're averse, you may find that you're so afraid of what's happened to your investments that you can't open your monthly statements. This only makes the situation worse, because you're averse to something that's unknown and nebulous. It's not even reality at that moment, since you're reacting to incomplete or imagined information.

Aversion often expresses itself irrationally, blowing things out of proportion. Someone who's experiencing aversion in its extreme form goes from seeing the ticker lose 500 points to thinking that a market collapse is inevitable, or that another Great Depression is around the corner and that they and their family will be destitute. If this sounds far-fetched, rest assured, it's not. I've worked with clients who could barely function in the fall of 2008 because they experienced such great anxiety from this aversion. It was only by tailoring the Mindfulness techniques to what they were experiencing, using special exercises, and through their diligent practice that they were able to regain their calmness and peace of mind.

Ignorance, Confusion, and Delusion

Together these three represent one hindrance. This hindrance is characterized by not seeing reality for what it is. Most people realize that they don't know what they don't know. However, people suffering with this hindrance believe they do know it all, and are often so convinced that they're correct that it's impossible to convince them that they might not have the right answer.

Ignorance arises as a result of beliefs or views that aren't founded on facts or correct information. It can also be indicative of a lack of clarity and a confused state of mind. Ignorance may be at fault when you make poor investment decisions because you don't know or employ solid financial planning principles, or you don't have a good understanding of the investments that make up your portfolio.

Confusion is closely linked to ignorance, and occurs when someone isn't fully aware of something, such as someone who doesn't grasp that stocks are included in the mutual funds they're investing in, even though this has been explained to them.

Delusion refers to maintaining inappropriate patterns. A deluded mind is often stuck in the past and uses the past to predict the future, such as someone who is maintaining spending habits that they can't afford. This could be because they still see themselves in a particular economic bracket, even though it's no longer their reality. In some cases, people in a delusional state believe they're deserving of things they can't afford, as if unrealistic material goods are somehow a birthright.

Like the other hindrances, ignorance, confusion, and delusion can cause great suffering when, inevitably, reality strikes—such as foreclosure on a property. The saying "ignorance is bliss" definitely has its limits.

Envy and Jealousy

Envy and jealousy are rooted in a place of deep insecurity, and refer to wanting what others have. People who suffer from this hindrance feel that somehow they're not good enough, but that if they could only get what another person has, they'll be equally worthwhile. This "keeping up with the Joneses" mindset presumes that self-esteem is inextricably linked with material possessions, status, looks, and connections.

Envy and jealousy often manifest themselves through spending beyond your means in order to buy a larger home, a boat, or another car; put an extension on the house; et cetera. When you fall victim to this hindrance, you feel a sense of incompleteness that you think can only be satiated when you obtain what someone else has, or intends to have. But the satisfaction is fleeting, if it exists at all, because someone else always has more than you do. As soon as you satisfy the first desire, another one creeps in and you're off in search of that thing, in a desperate attempt to maintain your sense of worthiness.

Envy and jealousy make you believe that satisfaction and fulfillment lie outside of yourself, that by your nature you're incomplete and something external is required to make you whole. You can see how it's a slippery slope: much like an addict who can never be satisfied, someone who is envious or jealous can never be satisfied.

Pride

Pride manifests in two ways—as superior and inferior pride. Superior pride says, "I am better than you," while inferior pride says, "You are better than me."

Those with superior pride need to win all the time in order to feel worthy. They'll go to great lengths to try to make others feel inferior—by reminding them of how smart they themselves are, how much money they have, how well connected they are, how much money they have made with their investments. But it's all a house of cards; in reality sufferers of this hindrance are saying, almost with every breath, "I'm better than you, *aren't I?*"

Conversely, those with inferior pride believe they can do no right. Everyone is smarter, faster, richer, luckier than they are. They often think of themselves as situational victims. They too experience insatiability, but in their case it's insatiable inferiority. They're often seen trying to associate with those who have superior pride because, by association, they're somewhat elevated in status. People who exhibit this tendency tend to be copycats and follow trends for fear of being left behind or sticking out. They can be vulnerable to investment fads or the latest hot tip.

DEALING WITH HINDRANCES

As we mentioned, everyone suffers from some of these hindrances from time to time. It's part of the human condition. However, if you find that you're so driven by any of these hindrances that it's affecting your quality of life, then you may wish to implement some changes. If you recognize that you're suffering from some of these but they're not having an adverse affect on you, then simply being aware of it can be enough to keep you out of trouble. Remember that without awareness you lose options, and are merely carried away by the moment. Stimulus and response have no gap, and you'll be forced to react rather than respond. We're encouraging you to make good decisions, not to be perfect. Making good decisions can help make your money work for you, rather than you becoming a slave to your money.

Unchecked hindrances tend to move you away from focus, clarity, and equanimity. One of the benefits of practising Mindfulness is that these hindrances, over time, begin to dissolve and eventually can wash away altogether. In chapter 2 we introduced the idea of purification. Hindrances are some of the patterns that can be purified by regular meditation practice. You'll find that when you look back after practising for some time you'll find that the things that really used to bother or worry you no longer have a hold on you at all. You'll wonder what's happened. You've practised, and maybe felt a little calmer and more at peace, but believed nothing unusual happened in your practice. But in hindsight you'll see how your life has been transformed.

As you continue practising you'll increasingly find that you're no longer driven, but rather you're motivated. Motivated to do things, to accomplish your goals. You're no less effective from this lack of drive. In fact, you'll be more effective because you'll be focused on what you want to achieve, clear about what you want to achieve, and equanimous (calmly accepting) about the outcome. Concerned that a lack of drive will make you less competitive and effective? Just watch Tiger Woods in action, or observe Phil Jackson coach the L.A. Lakers, and you'll see just how effective you can be without being slavish. Their meditation practice helps them to stay motivated to succeed rather than being driven to it. Being driven is generally associated with an insatiable craving which, over time, takes control over your mind. On the other hand, motivation keeps you focused and engaged toward your goals.

Remember that you can influence your behaviour, but not your results; trying to control situations usually backfires, and they end up controlling you. When you're fixated on controlling outcomes, you miss opportunities. You get stuck in the past or the future, and don't function with ease in the present moment—the only moment that truly exists. If you take care of this moment, of performing in it, the next one will take care of itself.

This is no different than creating a financial plan that's in line with your mission, needs, priorities, and goals, or staying actively focused, clear, and equanimous (balanced, rather than fighting with yourself), regardless of external influences (like market fluctuations). When you're mindful you remember how and when to seek advice, and are likely to make better decisions; unencumbered by worry or fear, you can respond with agility when required and stay put when required. Rather than being influenced by the herd who may be selling in a panic because surely the sky is falling, you're driven by your internal compass.

Mindfulness Exercise

Here is a meditation exercise that can be useful when you want to reflect upon any of the hindrances described, and what part they play in your life. Begin by relaxing yourself to the best of your ability. You can use the techniques described in chapter 3. Then ask yourself some or all of the following questions (you can reflect on one of these at a time or combine a couple into any given reflection):

- Is there anything that you're attached to, so much so that you say to yourself, "I won't/can't let go of this, no matter what"? It could be a possession, a belief, or something else. This may take the form of "If I were to lose 'X,' I'd be devastated."

- Is there anything that you have a deep aversion to? It could take the form of a huge fear or significant worry. It might be an aversion to your children not following the family tradition of becoming whatever (name the profession), or it could be an aversion to losing money in your portfolio. If the aversion to losing money is strong enough, you may wish to reconsider the level of risk in your portfolio.

- Has anyone you respect ever told you that you're not thinking clearly or that you're not basing your decisions on facts? This may be a sign that you're suffering from ignorance, confusion, and delusion.

- Do you ever experience envy and jealousy to the point where you purchase or do something just because someone else has or does it? Take the time to think about why you did it, especially if it really wasn't what you wanted. Have you ever gone into debt because you were trying to keep up with someone else?

- Are you constantly comparing yourself to others? Do you need the approval of others to feel worthwhile or do you need to be with others who may appear inferior to you in order to feel at ease?

In addition to reflecting upon these thoughts in meditation, try being aware during the course of your day. Begin by choosing one hindrance for a week, or even for a couple of days, and try to become aware when you exhibit it. For example, for a couple of days or a week, become aware when you exhibit attachment in your life. It could be in your professional life, at home, or on the golf course. Do nothing about what you discover, simply become aware of it. Your goal is to increase the awareness in your day-to-day life. Pay particular attention to your relationship with money. Do you exhibit any hindrances with money?

If you want to take it a step further and experience greater benefit, pay attention to what's happening in your subjective world (i.e., the Feel, Image, and Talk spaces) when you experience any of the hindrances very strongly. For example, if you experience great jealousy, make contact with Feel space, and locate it in your body. Is there an image on the visual screen? Is there talk in the Talk space that's carrying some commentary? As you know from chapter 3, you want to stay focused and concentrate on what's going on. You want to be clear and notice what's arising, and you want to surrender to it. In other words, you want to be equanimous. Don't resist it, because resisting can take the form of judging or justifying yourself; do neither of these. Just stay with it and have a full experience. This is how purification occurs.

To reiterate, the goal is not to become perfect and free from all of the hindrances. Rather, we're interested in experiencing life fully, to finding fulfillment, and minimizing, if not eliminating, suffering. Any of these hindrances that are allowed to go unchecked and get out of control can cause great suffering to both you and those around you. They'll also prevent you from finding fulfillment in life, since you'd be living primarily, if not exclusively, in the past and the future, while fulfillment only occurs in the present.

This exercise follows the same pattern as was described in chapter 3 of working with both a formal practice and strategies for Mindfulness in action. By doing both you can accelerate and deepen your Mindfulness skills.

Chapter 5

The Starting Point

Now that you've been introduced to the basics of Mindfulness meditation, we'll move on to look at the basics of financial planning and how the two complement one another. When you combine your heightened awareness, ability to focus on your true goals, and new sense of equanimity and acceptance of "what is" with sound financial planning basics, you'll find that you're better able to plan for a successful future and cope with any pitfalls along the way.

Most often, preparing a financial plan involves a trip to your banker, financial advisor, or planner, and the completion of a lot of forms. You'll be asked questions about your income, spending, current assets, and financial goals. These appear to be key questions, and yet often they are asked, answered, and entered into a computer program in the span of a short hour-long meeting. Then the printer spits out a financial plan mapping out your future.

During a standard financial planning meeting, you'll be asked to rank the following items as *very important*, *important*, *somewhat important*, or *unimportant*: capital growth, tax minimization, safety of capital, liquidity, income generation, leaving an estate, education, and income protection. Your answers are then used to create your plan. Well, who wouldn't want all of these things? We submit that these aren't really goals at all; rather, they're things that you would like to have happen to your money. But money is only a tool. We think that rather than focusing on what's going to happen to your money, you should focus on what's going to happen to you—how do you want to use the tool of money in your life?

Remember, Mindfulness is about training yourself to be in the present moment, free from glory or worry about the past and the future. By training yourself to be mindful, you will increasingly be able to experience concentration/focus, clarity, and equanimity. You'll be able to stay focused even when circumstances may have you waver from your goals. Clarity means that you will see reality for what it is, including your own emotions about money, uncertainty, et cetera. Being equanimous means being with what is, regardless of external pressures. Once you achieve this, you'll find that it's easier to decide what you truly want your life to look like, and to set financial goals that will help you achieve this. (Please refer to chapter 3 if you want some techniques to help you with concentration/focus, clarity, and equanimity.)

COUNTERPRODUCTIVE BEHAVIOUR PROFILES

Everyone knows that goal setting is important. Countless studies have proven that creating and writing down goals leads to success. After all, you're not going to get very far if you are drifting along without any particular direction or destination. But there are many traps when it comes to goal setting. As you read through the ones below, you may recognize the five hindrances—attachment; aversion; ignorance, confusion, and delusion; envy and jealousy; and pride—which we discussed in depth in chapter 4.

Each one of us experiences these hindrances to varying degrees. They may be more or less dominant at various points in our lives. Don't worry or feel guilty about experiencing these; it just means that you're human. Problems arise when you allow these hindrances to go unchecked and to mindlessly control your life. When this occurs, you're no longer living with purpose or living your true essence. Instead, you're allowing yourself to move further and further away from achieving true fulfillment. The end result of this can be only misery, and mental and physical stress.

As a reminder, here's a quick summary of what the hindrances represent in relation to your finances:

- Attachment is reflected in the unnatural attraction to material goods and social position, and to our views about money.

- Aversion is the fear of losing financial position or the approval/admiration of others.

- Ignorance, confusion, and delusion refer to believing in or being motivated by things that are not well founded.

This may be caused by erroneous or misguided beliefs, or simply a lack of accurate information.

- Envy and jealousy are self-explanatory. They refer to wanting what others have, and to being motivated by what others possess, regardless of whether it's truly of value to us.

- Pride can manifest itself in two ways: feelings of superiority or inferiority. Some people need to feel superior to others in order to feel self-worth. Others suffer from feeling inferior, and consequently they are motivated to overcome this by working to gain the approval of others.

Take a moment to reflect on any of these that currently apply to you. Doing so will put you in a position to make a choice as to whether or not you wish to be driven by these hindrances. Remember, we're not aiming to be perfect and eradicate these potential tendencies, but rather to be aware of them. With greater awareness, you'll be in a position to make mindful, conscious choices instead of being driven by unconscious patterns that may be controlling your life.

Below are the most common profiles that we've run into when meeting with clients over the years. Awareness of these will not only make it easier for you to discover your true goals, but will also make it easier to achieve those goals. We can't list them all, but do any of these sound familiar?

The Conspicuous Consumers

Many people seem on the surface to have it all—a house in a nice neighbourhood, a couple of cars, two or three vacations a year, private school for the kids. But once we delve a little deeper, often we find that these people are struggling to keep up the illusions. They are labouring under crushing debt and can't get ahead. Even so, they don't feel able to give up their material things, either because they would be embarrassed to admit that they were in difficulty, or because they feel entitled. Their neighbour/brother/colleague has these things, so why shouldn't they?

In the case of conspicuous consumers, you may recognize all five hindrances. Those in this category are living by someone else's standards. Living this life causes great anxiety and stress. Individuals in this category are never satisfied and never fulfilled. Their needs and desires become insatiable, because the standard—to keep up with others—is unattainable; there will always be someone else who has more.

The Postponers

Postponers tend to delay gratification, holding it off into the future. We have run into many people who have gone without for their entire working lives. They concentrated on working and saving as much as they could. Their goal was to accumulate enough money to relax and travel during their retirement years, so they worked overtime, went without holidays and new cars, et cetera. Sadly, all of that hard work takes a toll, and all too often illness or death prevents these dreams from coming true.

Additionally, circumstances change. For instance, grand-children often enter the picture around the same time that retirement takes place. Don't underestimate the pull that these little ones will have on you. We have clients (and even rela-tives) who scrimped and saved to buy a vacation property in a warm clime so they could enjoy retirement away from the snow and ice. But—you guessed it—once the time came to actually leave for an extended period, it was unimaginable. Too much family life would be missed.

Here we see the hindrances of attachment; aversion; and ignor-ance, confusion, and delusion. People become attached to a point of view. For instance, that it's better to save now and cash in later in life, as if they can predict what life might hold. Postponers are averse to not having enough in the future, and forgo quality of life in the present. And their ignorance, confu-sion, and delusion cause them to believe that they can predict their life in the future. These people are often bitter and sad in later life, when despite all of their planning, the future doesn't turn out as they expected.

The Pleasers

These people don't know what their own goals are. While they may think that they do, when we examine things closely, it turns out that they have been living someone else's dream. This can happen for a number of reasons. For example, children try to live up to their parents' expectations. If they don't have the best of everything, their parents make them feel guilty. The parents feel that they provided every advantage to the kids, so why aren't they succeeding? Sometimes it's a spouse who imposes his or her wishes on their partner, without allowing the other partner to have fair input. And sometimes it's society's input that creates havoc. Witness the 2008 sub-prime mortgage crisis in the U.S. So many of the people caught up in this mess never had a hope of repaying their loans. Deep down they must have known that, but they were seduced by the American dream of owning a home. Unfortunately, home ownership became a nightmare, partly because they were trying to live someone else's dream.

All five hindrances apply to this category. Pleasers don't live their own lives. They are constantly ill at ease, and may not be sure why. Despite achieving all of the goals that are expected of them, there is still a sense that there should be more to life. They tend to feel that they don't know their true purpose.

Pleasers are attached to the views of others, averse to not pleasing, deluded about what matters to them, often envious of those who are not living by the standards of others, and can experience both superior and inferior pride. They may feel superior pride because they often accomplish great things, but at the same time have a sense of inferiority as they fear not being able to maintain their pace or success. They can feel like imposters. This causes a tremendous amount of stress.

The Hoarders

Hoarders often grew up in relatively difficult circumstances, and fear running out of money. All their lives they have worked hard to accumulate a nest egg so that they can feel secure and enjoy life. Yet, despite having plenty of money, they're reluctant to spend it. They clip coupons, buy dented cans; if they eat out at all, it's only at the 5 p.m. "blue plate special." Because their goal—to have "enough" money—is based in fear, they will never be able to achieve it. How will what they have ever be enough? They become so attached to their money that they can't spend it. Every dip in their bank balances, either because of spending or market downturns, causes them great stress. Even though they have money, it doesn't give them pleasure or peace of mind. So what was the point of all the years of hard work and saving?

Hoarders experience great suffering on a daily basis. They are averse to not having enough. They become attached to everything they have, and are afraid it might be taken away. They also experience confusion and delusion about what really motivates them and what's at the root of this unfortunate obsession. The reality is that they experience a sense of insecurity and attempt to protect themselves by accumulating as much as they can. They think that the more belongings they have, the more secure they'll feel. Unfortunately, what they lack is internal, and as a result, the need for protection and security will be insatiable.

The only way to appease this need is to develop a clear connection and awareness of who they truly are and how their hindrances have affected their view of reality. Chapter 3 contained information on how to develop internal security and decrease suffering.

Remember not to panic if you do find yourself falling victim to one of these typical pitfalls. We are not saying that you have to change, but rather that you may wish to reflect on your choices and whether this is the life you want to continue living. Mindfulness is about making conscious choices, and about being clear about the choices we make and what drives us.

YOUR MISSION STATEMENT

We certainly agree that goal setting is crucial to financial success. However, the usual approach is to set your goals with a view to the future, most often retirement. We find that it's better to approach your finances by working backward from your future. We suggest that instead of starting *with* the end, you start *at* the end. The idea is to start with the end in mind.

In order to discover your true goals, you'll need to examine the reasons why you want these things. As discussed, many people wind up pursuing things for the wrong reason. They fall prey to familial or societal pressures, and end up working their whole lives for things that, in the end, aren't that important to them. But, now that you're aware of some of these problems, you're better equipped to be successful.

So, let's get to work. At the end of the process, you'll have determined what you want to achieve with your life. This will make it easier for you to establish a mission statement for your life. Once you have done that, goal setting will be much easier for you. All you have to do is set goals (financial and otherwise) that bring you closer to achieving your mission statement.

Remember we said we were going to start with the end in mind? Well, here it goes. Start by going forward in time. Imagine that you have reached the end of a fulfilling life (don't worry, you don't have to be on your deathbed, you can be on a beach chair in Maui if you like). Look back over your life and describe it. How have you spent your time? What have you achieved? What are you most proud of? What kind of person have you become? Consider your life at that moment, and notice what has been most important in your life. Remember, for this exercise you are the *only* judge and jury; this way you'll ensure that these are things that truly matter to you. Use this information to help you with the following gap analysis exercise.

Gap Analysis Exercise:

Step 1

Write down the kind of person you hope to become and the most important things you hope to have achieved by the end of your life.

Step 2

Write down the things that you have achieved to date. Are you the kind of person you wish to be? Determine which of your achievements are in line with your own priorities, and which are a result of societal or familial pressures.

Step 3

Examine the information in step 2 and consider if you're living life primarily based on your own priorities or on outside expectations. Make note of any discrepancies in step 2. This is the present gap in your life. If there are significant discrepancies, changes will need to be made to achieve a fulfilling end state. At this point, equanimity is of critical importance. You must accept yourself as you are right now, without judgment. If this step has revealed that you're not living life the way you wish or that you're not currently the person you wish to be, take this as valuable information to help you make changes in your life. Whatever you've discovered "it is what it is." Don't resist or struggle with what arises in your Feel/Image/Talk spaces; simply allow it to arise without interference. This is what it is to be equanimous. From here you can make changes to those areas of your life that are within your control.

Step 4

Examine your responses in the previous steps and determine what you need to change in your life. Ask yourself if and when you are willing to make these changes.

Step 5

Now determine what you need to do over the years to achieve a fulfilling life. Even if steps 2 and 3 show that presently your achievements are in line with what's important to you and that you're satisfied with the person you are, you'll need to continue to plan for the future. What are the major things you need to do to keep you on track or to achieve significant future goals?

Step 6

Create your mission statement by describing your main purpose in life. This will help you to determine how to spend your time in the future, and which opportunities to take advantage of and which to turn down because they lead you away from your mission statement and from living life "on purpose."

The result of this work will be a clearer picture of what matters most to you and how different it may (or may not) be from the present course in your life. This will enable you to be strategic and proactive about how you live your life, rather than simply allow life to happen to you. The gap analysis (understanding the difference between these two things) is necessary in order to give you a sense of what you need to alter in your life. Some of you may already be living lives in line with your true essence, but if that is not the case, you'll need to make some choices. You need to make sure you're comfortable in your own skin, and give yourself a sense that you're leading a life well lived.

If your gap analysis reveals that changes should be made, reflect on what you will need to adjust in order to accomplish your true goals. When thinking about what your true goals may be, consider the circumstances when you have experienced real and sustained happiness and when you have felt the calmest. Of course, these circumstances can apply to both your personal and professional lives.

Living mindfully does not mean living in poverty (we like material things as much as the next person), but it's also not necessarily a case of saving or spending the most money. There are no "the one who dies with the most toys wins" bumper stickers here. Living mindfully doesn't entail living by society's standards of success, but rather by your own internal compass. Try to live according to true north within yourself.

Once you have done the gap analysis of what matters to you, you're ready to develop your own mission statement. A mission statement can be used as a litmus test for all you do. For example, Maria's mission statement is "to contribute to positively transforming the lives of individuals and organizations by helping them help themselves through Mindfulness." Your mission statement will allow you to assess every opportunity or decision you make in relation to what matters most to you.

But before you finalize your mission statement, you may wish to meditate on it. You can use one of the techniques from chapter 3—Creating Positive Outcomes—to "experience" your new mission statement. As we described in chapter 3, place some awareness in Feel space, Image space, and Talk space. In Image space, create an image or images of yourself living in line with your mission statement. Be as clear as you possibly can. You may also wish to create internal talk that supports your image. Repeat the word(s) or phrase to yourself at a leisurely and rhythmic pace. Then become aware of what's happening, if anything, in your Feel centres or in the body globally. Now that you're wearing that mission, what's your experience of it? Does it generate something positive within you? Is it exciting? Is it worthy of you? Let your inner wisdom inform and guide you.

At this point you may realize that you're pleased with the mission statement you have created or you may think there's more work to be done. If there's still work to be done, follow the process described in this chapter once again until you're satisfied. It's worth the effort; after all, it's your life to live.

Once you have created your mission statement and a vision of the life you want to live, setting your financial goals will be much easier. Now you're better equipped to answer those questions at the start of most financial plans. You will simply have to make the decisions and set the goals that allow you to live your version of a life well lived, both now and in the future.

Chapter 6

The Financial Plan

In chapter 5 you began to give some thought to what your goals are, and to what you'd like to achieve with your life by creating your personal mission statement. This chapter will show you how a computer-generated forecast—your financial plan—can tell you if you have the resources to live out your dreams exactly as you envision or if you need to make changes, either to your financial situation or to your goals.

A financial plan is simply an illustrative tool. In the old days before computerization it was an expensive and time-consuming process to have one prepared, and extremely awkward to make even the simplest change. Annual surpluses and deficits needed to be calculated and entered by hand. Now financial planning tools are commonplace and quite accessible. In fact, most financial institutions offer free financial plans as part of their service. The illustrations and outcomes are presented in a graphic form that's easy to interpret and useful for reviewing various scenarios. This is an ideal development for mindful clients and advisors, offering an easy way to work with data so clients can feel empowered to explore multiple scenarios and ask seemingly outlandish questions of themselves and their planner. Don't feel restricted to the questions of what might happen if you save $300 a month or if you receive dividends instead of interest from your investments; use the programs to their capacity and incorporate your mission statement and goals into the plan.

The financial plan is not only the first step in the financial planning process, it's also the home base that clients and their advisors should return to and refer to when working with the other areas covered in this book. Everything that happens in your life that may have a financial impact easily can be illustrated there.

Before we get into the details of a typical financial plan, take a moment to write down the mission statement that you developed in chapter 5. In addition, write down your three most important goals/hopes and your three biggest fears. In most cases your financial planner will be able to translate the impact that these goals and fears will have on your financial future. Our goal in this chapter is to show you how to structure a plan (or have one structured for you) to reach your goals/hopes while avoiding your fears. As you work through the information in this chapter, pay attention to your subjective spaces (Feel, Image, and Talk) and remember that if Feel is strong enough, it will drive behaviour. Being aware of what's occurring in the spaces means that you're more likely to remain in control of your mind, rather than being hijacked by its runaway thoughts.

THE FINANCIAL PLAN

The typical plan will require you to input the following information:

- Your family's personal data, including birth dates, address, and so on

- Expenses—include current information, plus if you expect them to change at various points in your life you should indicate this too (as a rough guide, you could estimate that your expenses in retirement will be 70% of what you spend while you're working)

- Long-term (and retirement) savings—once your debt has been paid off and you've accumulated an emergency fund equivalent to six months worth of expenses, you could begin to save a portion of your income toward funding your goals

- Retirement dates for you and your spouse

- Education details and estimated cost and dates of attendance for dependants

- Wills, including date of last review and where they are located

- Incomes—current and forecast

- Pensions—current and forecast

- Personal assets—include house, cottage, artwork, and so on; if you see any of these as investments you are willing to sell later for use as investment capital, then enter them as investment assets:

- Investment assets—include the original cost and present value of the investments and include assumptions for the rate of return and the standard deviation for each investment (standard deviation is used to measure risk and we discuss it in more detail later in this chapter)

- Tax-advantaged investments (retirement savings)

- Insurance—list details about the owner, face value, amount of death benefit, premium cost, type (term, whole life, or universal), and enter the current cash value, if any

The data entry summary page will detail everything that was entered into the plan, including both data that you provided and the assumptions used by the program. Check it carefully for accuracy. While mundane, this attention to detail will give you more confidence in the final output.

Several of these areas are key, and we discuss them in more detail below.

Retirement Dates

In today's economic reality, you should consider your retirement date a moving target. Our advice is not to become too attached to a specific age or date. While you may feel that you can work forever, the reality is that as you grow older you may become tired and frustrated. Give yourself a factor of safety by testing out different retirement dates on the financial plan. Use five years before and five years after your hoped-for date, and see what the effect is on the amount you'll need to save and the amount you'll have available to spend.

Pensions

In recent years, pensions have gone through, and are continuing to go through, a major transition. In the past, companies took on the risk of providing a *defined benefit* to their members. This is a stated monthly pension income that's calculated based on years of service, often with some indexing to inflation. Most government, public service, and teacher pension plans are still designed like this. In defined benefit pension plans, in essence the companies take on all the market risk in funding the pension. If you have one of these pensions, your pension booklet will have a pension calculator in it. Combine the formula with your hoped-for retirement age and from that calculate your pension. Financial planning software often has a function to calculate it for you.

The other type of pension plan is a *money purchase* plan (or defined contribution plan). With these plans, your pension benefit isn't defined based on your years of service, it's based on the performance of the underlying investments. You contribute to a money purchase plan on a regular basis, and often employers do too, although more recently many have been cutting out their contributions to these plans. You'll be provided with a choice of investment funds into which your contributions are invested. Your firm may have some fiduciary responsibility to help you with this choice. If you have a money purchase plan, enter the details on your financial plan as if this were a tax-sheltered retirement account.

Spending Needs/Budget

We focus heavily on this area because people are often wildly wrong in their spending estimates. There are two ways to calculate spending needs: the quick estimate and a full budget.

Many advisors simply give in to the groans and protestations of clients and recommend estimating your spending needs using a rule of thumb. This involves looking at your assets and determining how much you add or subtract from them in the year (excluding major, one-time purchases). Subtract this number from your net income and you have an estimate of spending (or overspending) needs.

Here are a couple of simple examples:

> Bank account balance on January 1 is $10,000.
>
> Bank account balance on December 31 is $20,000,
>
> for a gain of $10,000.
>
> Net income after taxes is $90,000.
>
> Deduct gain from income:
>
> $90,000 − $10,000 = $80,000 in expenses.
>
> *OR*

Bank account balance on January 1 is $10,000.

Bank account balance on December 31 is $0,

for a loss of $10,000.

Net income after taxes is $90,000.

Add loss to income:

$90,000 + $10,000 = $100,000 in expenses.

If you truly can't bear the thought of making up and tracking a budget, then this method will have to do. However, taking the time to detail and track your expenses in a full budget is a great opportunity to get a real grasp on your spending situation, and it will make your plan significantly better. There are lots of computerized budget templates available, or if you like you can use the budget template we provide in appendix B. We think you'll find the results of a full budget to be a real eye-opener.

Taking the time to update your budget whenever you review your plan will give you an accurate number for your spending and highlight areas you can, and probably should, change. This difference between needs and income is critical to your future. Here's an example of how an apparently simple spending decision will be greatly affected by how familiar you are with your budget and will greatly affect your financial future.

A person making $200,000 a year would like to spend $5,000 each year on a vacation for his family of four. Seems simple and affordable, right? After all it's only 2.5% of his employment

income. However, a review of the annual budget, shown
below, indicates that this isn't the case.

Income	$200,000
Income taxes and property taxes	90,000
Employee cost of benefits	5,000
Mortgage and property maintenance	48,000
Food and entertainment	24,000
Car leases, maintenance, gas, insurance	18,000
Country club fees and expenses	12,000
Clothing	5,000
Total	**($ 2,000)**

Running the numbers shows that the family actually can't afford
to take a vacation—they're already operating at a deficit. What
if they haven't been keeping track and they just assume they can
afford it? How much will a one-time vacation cost? Assume that
the family uses a credit card to pay for the trip. From the budget
above we realize they can't even afford to make the minimum
monthly payments of 2.5%. Often this can be the start of a debt
cycle that involves borrowing from somewhere else to make
these minimum payments. Even if they do manage to make
the minimum payments without incurring more debt, at 18.5%
interest this week-long vacation will still take them approximately 26 years to pay for, and cost more than $7,000 in interest,
plus the original $5,000. Remember, that's the minimum it will

cost them; if they have to borrow to cover these payments, the situation will be much gloomier.

Imagine if the family continued on, ignorant of their financial situation, and kept taking these seemingly inexpensive vacations for the next 10 years. The total cost, including interest, would be close to $120,000. Because they aren't mindful of their finances, the family would be left wondering why they can never get ahead financially, and would suffer from the stress of having to work longer hours for more years in order to gather money for retirement.

You might think that as the debt accumulates they would simply stop taking vacations. However, the easy access to credit over recent years has helped to disguise the problem and has fuelled an explosion of consumer debt (we talk more about credit in chapter 9). The hindrances we discussed in chapter 4 also play a key role in the accumulation of debt. Left unchecked, they can spiral out of control and expenditures begin to be perceived as necessities rather than luxuries. In the past, inflation helped people extract themselves from the debt cycle. As homes and incomes ballooned in value, it was easy to free up cheap capital, people felt safe in the knowledge that incomes would increase yearly, and homes were an increasingly valuable asset that could be used to bail them out if things went wrong. Of course, now we are facing a different and rather less hopeful situation.

Deferred Gratification

Adding an element of deferred gratification to your purchases is a sign of maturity as an adult and consumer. To be truly successful you must learn to defer. Immature children (and immature adults) often feel a deep sense of disappointment and anxiety when they can't get what they want *right now*. There's an underlying sense that they'll never get it; they feel that if they don't get the item right now, the opportunity will be lost. It's important to learn to recognize these urges within yourself so you can gain control over them. Next time you experience an urge, work with the Internal Awareness technique. Make contact with Feel, Image, or Talk space (see chapter 3 to review this technique) and don't resist or interfere with what you experience, simply become aware of it and experience it fully. Remember that by applying equanimity and accepting what arises you'll experience pain, but not suffering. If you persist you'll eventually experience "purification," which is the dissolution of negative patterns. With practice, your cravings will dissolve and no longer negatively impact your behaviour.

Try this experiment so you can get used to the feeling. Take a piece of chocolate cake and place it in front of you. (This is assuming you like chocolate cake, but feel free to substitute as necessary.) Enjoy the smell of it and the anticipation of eating it. Bring a forkful to your lips, but don't eat it. Instead, put it in the refrigerator. The Feel that you experience at the moment is similar to the Feel you experience when you have a craving for purchases—remember and watch out for it. You'll know that you're back in control the next time you feel the urge to buy something but decide to wait a few days. (This will become easier as you locate Feel in your body and continue to experience it without resistance.) Often you'll forget about the item entirely because the impulse will have passed. Unchecked, Feel is likely to impair your judgment and cause you to make poor decisions.

When you experience cravings, it's worth reflecting on which, if any, of the five hindrances are playing a role (see chapter 4 for more information on hindrances). Be as objective as you can when you consider whether attachment; aversion; ignorance, confusion, and delusion; envy and jealousy; and/or pride are impacting your cravings and decisions.

Many of my clients are good at deferring gratification, often showing foresight and budgeting skill by assigning income generated from a particular investment stream as their special "fun money" income. This allows them to enjoy their purchases without having to worry about the effects on their financial plan. Many times a stock or group of stocks left by a parent or relative through their estate can be used in this way to give a constant stream of lifetime pleasure.

If you have something special you really love to do—a weekend spa trip, dinner and fine wine with good friends, or a vacation—try working out what level of cash flow you'll need to pay for it. Tuck aside either a lump sum that you have available now or build one up with regular savings, and wait for a good time to purchase a single stock or small group of high-dividend-paying stocks that will generate the income required for your adventures. Set this aside from your assets before you put your overall financial plan together. Be aware that recently we've had some great opportunities to buy blue-chip stocks with dividend yields at all-time highs, and there'll likely be a few more.

Money and Kids—the Parental Mind

Often people will tell me "I wish that they'd teach this financial planning stuff to kids." This comment always makes me smile. More often than not, adults are the ones who need help with their finances, not kids. The budget is the key to your financial success or failure, and most kids are masters at budgeting and managing their money—it seems like it's in their DNA. I've noticed through the years that they often plot and scheme at great length to determine how to manage within their allowance (the real name for your discretionary spending).

As a parent you have a duty and responsibility to encourage and foster this trait in your children. You can start by simply not giving in to your own need for gratification (or simply for peace and quiet) by always being the good guy and pulling out the magic credit card to make all the kids' wishes come true (or your own, for that matter). Teaching them to wait and save for things they really want is a valuable lesson. If you don't, you risk sowing the seeds of financial trouble for your children. And remember, if things go really badly for them, they could end up on your doorstep with your grandkids in tow, which may hamper your own well-laid retirement plans. Always set aside an area of your budget, such as vacations and charitable giving, and allow all of the family members to share in the decision-making process for that portion. This will help to encourage a lifetime of good habits.

Budgeting can seem overwhelming and nitpicky, but take heart: small changes in spending levels will make a huge difference in your financial forecast. Your financial plan will illustrate just how well being mature with your money will pay off in the long run.

THE RESULTS

Once you've supplied the necessary information and are satisfied that it's been entered accurately, you can focus on how all this data will actually affect your net worth. Are your assets going to increase in value? Are you going to run out of money before you die? Hold on to your seat, because you're about to find out. A picture is worth a thousand words, and the graphics produced by your planning program will help you clearly understand your situation. Your financial planner may keep drawing you back to the spreadsheets and details, but ignore them for now; just look at the big picture to begin with. The financial plan can generate different graphs, but the key one to focus on at this stage is the net worth graph. It might look something like this (if you're lucky).

Graph 6.1: Net Worth

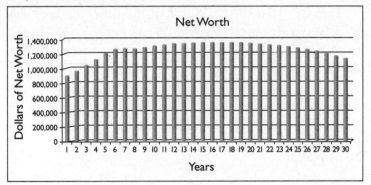

Welcome to Monte Carlo

You had to know that it couldn't be that easy—plug in some numbers, save every year, and voila, you magically have enough to achieve your goals. Now it's time to face the reality of luck and chance with your investments, and to see how it may affect your financial future. Welcome to the casino.

Remember that while stock and bond markets offer fairly predictable returns over the long term, their movements up and down on a year-to-year basis potentially can destroy your finances. This variation from the average return of an investment is called *standard deviation*. Essentially, standard deviation measures the level of risk or volatility in an investment.

For example, suppose a portfolio of stocks has averaged a 9% return over the long term and it has a standard deviation of 17. Suppose also that two-thirds of the time, the portfolio will offer returns in the range of 9% plus or minus 1 level of standard deviation. In this case, then, the returns could be anywhere from +26% to −8%. That leaves the other one-third of the time. In this case the portfolio will offer returns in the range of 9% plus or minus 2 levels of standard deviation, or anywhere from +43% to −25%. And be warned, approximately 5% of the time (or once every 20 years), there's a chance that the portfolio will swing even more widely away from the average.

So, how can this randomness have such a great effect on a portfolio? Consider this example:

Tom and Jim are brothers. Tom graduates from college one year before Jim. Upon their respective graduations, Dad loans each of them $100,000 to get them started in life. He charges them no interest, but expects to be repaid $25,000 each year over four years. The boys don't like to pay investment fees, so they both decide to invest their capital into aggressive index funds. The annual returns on the funds then follow this pattern:

Tom	+25%	−25%	+25%	−25%	Simple average return 0%
Jim	−25%	+25%	−25%	+25%	Simple average return 0%

END RESULTS FOR TOM:

Year 1

$100,000 grows by 25% for a total at year-end of $125,000. Repays Dad $25,000 for a net total of $100,000 in his investment account.

Year 2

$100,000 drops by 25% for a total at year-end of $75,000. Repays Dad $25,000 for a net total of $50,000 in his investment account.

Year 3

$50,000 grows by 25% for a total at year-end of $62,500. Repays Dad $25,000 for a net total of $37,500 in his investment account.

Year 4

$37,500 drops by 25% for a total at year-end of $28,125. Repays Dad the final $25,000 and is left with a profit of $3,125.

END RESULTS FOR JIM:

Year 1

$100,000 drops by 25% for a total at year-end of $75,000. Repays Dad $25,000 for a net total of $50,000 in his investment account.

Year 2

$50,000 grows by 25% for a total at year-end of $62,500. Repays Dad $25,000 for a net total of $37,500 in his investment account.

Year 3

$37,500 drops by 25% for a total at year-end of $28,125. Repays Dad $25,000 for a net total of $3,125 in his investment account.

Year 4

$3,125 grows by 25% for a total at year-end of $3,906.25. Gives this amount to Dad, and still owes him $21,093.75.

Graph 6.2: Tom and Jim Scenario

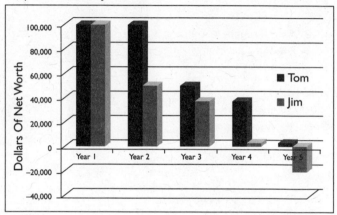

Even though Tom and Jim both had the exact same average return of zero, there is a $24,218.75 difference between the $3,125 profit realized by Tom and the $21,093.75 debt incurred by Jim. Because Tom started in a year when the markets went up, he finished with cash in his pocket, while Jim started in a down market and finished in debt to his father.

As this example shows, timing and circumstance can play a key role in financial outcomes. Mindfulness is helpful in dealing with this fact. Applying equanimity to the situation will allow you to accept what you can't control and to change what you can from a place of calmness, focus, and clarity. When you are mindful, you'll be able to make better decisions without getting caught up in a vicious cycle of fear, blame, and judgment. In our example, Jim would likely experience significant Feel, and without Mindfulness training he would likely be caught up in endless worry, fear, anger, blame, and a whole host of other unproductive states. With Mindfulness training Jim would be aware of the seriousness of the situation, but would be able to apply the Internal Awareness technique and track what was arising in his Feel, Image, and Talk spaces. From a place of awareness he would be able to maintain control of his mind rather than being controlled by it, and would be able to make clear decisions. As noted in chapter 2, the more you practise the techniques, the more likely it is that you can widen the gap between stimulus and response, which will allow you to make better decisions and exercise more sound judgment. Often it's in the gap that you'll find a solution.

Monte Carlo simulations give you a more realistic picture of what may happen with your investments. They take the average rate of return for your investments and randomize the order in which you earn these rates of return. The simulations utilize standard deviation to measure how the performance of an investment might deviate from the average of other investments in the same category. We've included standard deviation (volatility) with the estimated returns from graph 6.1 (Net Worth), and show the new results below.

Graph 6.3: Net Worth with Monte Carlo Simulation

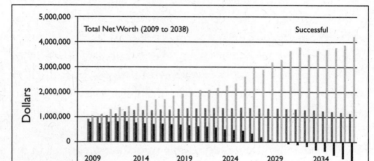

As you can see, with the current asset mix and level of spending there's a real risk of failure with this plan—that means the client running out of money. It's critical to be aware of the odds of your portfolio failing either from assuming too much risk or from settling for too little return. Even with identical average returns and an identical portfolio structure, the client who starts investing with generally positive years will have a better experience than the client with negative returns in the early years. Therefore it's critical to include standard deviation in your financial plan.

Below are examples of rates of return and the historical standard deviations that a typical North American could use in a computerized financial plan based on local markets. Your advisor and his firm will also have suggestions. Remember that these are simply approximations. Be prepared to adapt your plan on an annual basis.

Sample return on stocks	9%		Standard deviation	17%
Sample return on bonds	6%		Standard deviation	6%
Sample return on cash	4%		Standard deviation	0%
Inflation	2%			

YOUR PLAN

As you can see it's important for you to take an active role in the financial planning process. Partnering with your advisor is critical. Both you and your advisor need to be aware of your risk tolerance and your goals (the mission statement you developed in chapter 5 will be helpful in determining your goals).

Before worrying too much about how the details of Monte Carlo simulations and standard deviations apply to you, it's a good idea to determine if you actually need to take any risk within your portfolio. First, try a simple experiment. Take your portfolio and eliminate all the risk by putting it into cash or equivalents. Do you need to reduce your spending to avoid running out of money? By how much? Could you live comfortably with this spending level? Will it meet your estate goals? Will inflation eat up your capital? For some people this could be a great, worry-free portfolio.

As you consider the options for your portfolio, keep your personal mission statement and the five hindrances in mind, and try this exercise. Take the time to tune in to the Feel, Image, and Talk space (you may wish to review the Internal Awareness section in chapter 3). What's going on in these three spaces? Remember that, if they're left unchecked, the physical sensations associated with emotion in the Feel space will drive your behaviour. If they are unchecked, you potentially may be driven by fear, worry, or the desire to accumulate material goods, and will make poor decisions. Allow yourself to experience what's going on in these spaces without judging yourself. Apply equanimity to whatever you're experiencing (remember, this means accepting whatever's arising without resistance). This is very empowering and will allow you to develop your plan from a place of clarity and to focus on what matters most to you.

If the portfolio you try doesn't meet your needs, adjust the program to a balanced portfolio of 60% stocks and 40% bonds. Does this work? Keep adjusting until you find a portfolio asset mix and a spending level you can live comfortably with. An experienced Certified Financial Planner (CFP) often will know right away the mix that will work best for you, but it can still be interesting to play with the program to see what your options are.

You may also find it useful to use the Creating Positive Outcomes technique from chapter 3. Refer back to chapters 3 and 5 if you need clarification on the technique. Begin by creating an image of yourself living comfortably within your means. Imagine you have created a financial plan and you are well able to afford the things you are doing, imagine where you are living and how you are spending your money. You're at ease, have peace of mind, and are experiencing fulfillment in your life. Now create internal talk that supports what you've visualized. Repeat it to yourself over and over again at a leisurely pace for 10 minutes (or more, whatever's comfortable for you). If you're experiencing pleasant sensations in the body as a result of these positive visualisations and internal talk, encourage them to grow. This will help you to move your life in that direction. Remember that this is not an unrealistic dream, it's your future. Imagine positive outcomes that include fulfillment, comfortable risk-taking based on your level of tolerance, and financially responsible behaviour. Make a note to yourself at the end of the meditation so you remember what you experienced.

Chapter 7

Portfolio Construction

Once you and your advisor have created a plan and deter-mined an initial asset allocation that works to meet your goals, you'll need to begin choosing the actual investments. In this chapter we discuss the component parts of a portfolio and why, when combined, they can work together to reduce risk while maintaining return. We will also use this chapter to give you an understanding of the basics of investments, so that you can maintain focus and continue to make good, confident deci-sions even when things seem to be going the wrong way or when you're overcome by contrary suggestions.

It's important to review your mission statement at this stage. Remember that one of the reasons you developed it was so that you'd be able to assess opportunities and options as they arise. A great opportunity that's inconsistent with your mission statement isn't really an opportunity at all, because accepting it would take you off course. Your goal is to make financial (and life) decisions that are important and meaningful to you, so be sure to keep the five hindrances in mind and avoid fall-ing victim to societal pressures.

As you meet with your advisor to discuss the options available to you, do your best to remain in the present moment. Listen mindfully to the information being presented, and resist the temptation to get caught up in your own thoughts (chapter 8 has more information on Mindful listening). It's important to your success that from the very beginning you understand your strategy and investments. During the recent market crisis, many people experienced the awful feeling of trying to under stand their investments while things were going awry and they were blinded by panic. During the market correction in 1987, I was a less experienced advisor, and hadn't yet learned the skills necessary to listen mindfully to clients or to encourage them to become mindful of their situations. I was astounded when clients who had nodded wisely through a three-hour work-shop and several personal meetings with me called me after the market began dropping and said something like "I'm glad I'm in mutual funds, and not stocks" or "Why didn't we stay in GICs?" It was as if they thought that their investments had mystically appeared in their portfolio while they were sleeping. We had both failed in our communication strategy. Remember that you and your advisor are a team, and you shouldn't rely on him or her to manage and keep an eye on things without any contribution from you.

In order to successfully implement your investment strategy, you must take the time to become confident in your know-ledge and the route you've chosen. If you don't, you risk falling into the trap of chasing the "next big idea," which is a close cousin of the "I don't want to be left out" mindset. The other potential danger is giving up, throwing your hands in the air, closing your mind, believing "I'm not smart or sophisticated enough to understand this," and abdicating the responsibility of choosing the investments to your advisor. Both these scenarios are contrary to the goal of achieving clarity and equanimity with your investment portfolio and your overall financial situation.

Approaching your investment portfolio with clarity and equanimity is important because it will help you make wise decisions in the face of adversity. For example, it allows you to take in financial or economic news and have a good sense of how it will affect your portfolio without having to run to the computer and check your accounts. Consider that I don't look at each client's portfolio every day; it simply wouldn't be possible. However, because I'm mindful I'm able to be aware of how news affects my clients in general and, if I'm talking to an individual client, how it affects them specifically. I also have a good general sense of how investments are performing, without having to do a full analysis (although naturally I do full analyses prior to scheduled meetings or when questions arise that warrant further investigation).

We believe that your portfolio should include only investments that you completely understand. You need to know what they are, how they move, and where to find information about them, should you become confused or have questions. Here is a simple example of how keeping things simple and maintaining

Mindfulness can help you. Imagine that your portfolio is 50% stocks and 50% bonds. You're watching television and hear that stocks dropped 3% and bonds rose 1%. You can quickly estimate that your portfolio dropped 2%. Automatically, your mind asks you to worry about what's happening; however, because you have a calm understanding of your situation, you're able to be aware of the effect of the market movements without the usual foggy anxiety. You're familiar with your portfolio composition and workings, so you can take consolation from knowing that you generated income this month from dividends and interest being paid into the account. You know that a 2% drop isn't pleasant and may cause some temporary pain, but certainly no ongoing suffering. This ability to take in stimuli and then rationally and quickly see how they affect you personally will become habitual over time. Eventually this habit will help you to break the cycle of rumination and worry about your finances. Remember—the mind is a trickster, and it will do anything to keep you engaged with it and trapped in a fantasy world of past regrets and future fears.

BUILDING BLOCKS

Investor Psychology

The Zen attitude of a beginner's mind can be useful in all aspects of financial planning, and with portfolio management in particular. *Beginner's mind* is a way of looking at everything as if you're discovering it for the first time, as an enthusiastic and excited child would. Do this by examining every preconceived notion you have relating to investing and portfolio management. Start by saying, "I know nothing about this, so why do I believe it's true?" Think about the answer. Perhaps you heard it from an expert—either in the classroom, on TV, in a news article, book, or website. Do you know these people? Is their experience and knowledge current, or was it developed at a different time and under a different set of circumstances?

Remember that the downturn we recently experienced came at a time when risk management and computer-based modelling appeared to have reached new heights of sophistication and brilliance. As the market neared its peak there was even talk that the risk premium—the extra return you receive for investing in stocks rather than risk-free investments—was too high based on the actual level of risk.

Keep these other examples in mind as you listen to the current hot expert:

- The collapse of Long-Term Capital in the late 1990s, a company managed by the smartest and most highly qualified people of their day (clearly an example of smart people being overtaken by unexpected events)

- The talk of the "new paradigm" in investing before the dot-com market collapse in 2000

- The Asian financial crisis in 1997

- The silver collapse in 1980

All of the significant market downturns and crashes have been exacerbated by the wise words of "experts." At the same time as they're discredited, new experts rise from the ashes and the cycle begins again. One way to avoid being sucked in by all the hype and mania is to maintain beginner's mind. When you do this, you'll be able to take a step back and question what's going on rather than blindly following the latest craze. Remember that securities trade on a market and, just like when you go to the supermarket, you should examine the labels before buying to make sure the product is right for you.

While it's easy to get swept up in the madding crowd and allow fear and greed to take over your decisions, realize that if you do you're taking your wealth too seriously and giving it power over you. If you become attached to your investments in an unhealthy way, managing your portfolio will only drive you crazy. If you imagine that you need your wealth to give you status or you use it as a tool to control your family, you risk panicking when it looks like you'll lose money or becoming greedy when you see an opportunity to gain more power. Keep your money in perspective so you can make better decisions about it; it shouldn't sit first on your priority list. My priorities, in order, are:

1. Spiritual and mental health
2. Physical health for me and my family
3. Time
4. Opportunity to help others
5. Money

In setting your own priorities, remember that a bad set of results from your doctor is much worse than a bad set of results from your portfolio. In the same way that it's hard to cheat an honest man, it's hard to get caught up in the frenzy and make risky decisions when your life and attitude toward money are in balance and harmony.

The Investment Trinity

Because a basic knowledge of your investments and why they make up your portfolio is critical, in this section we review the three core categories of investments: cash, bonds, and stocks. While other types of investments exist, we believe that sticking with these three is the best way to create a mindful portfolio. Including exotic derivative strategies, for example, will make your plan almost impossible to rely upon. We believe that an investment needs to have three attributes to make it suitable for a mindful portfolio:

1. A history that's long enough to provide an estimate of future rates of return, relative to inflation

2. A track record of volatility that can be used to calculate its standard deviation

3. Simplicity; remember that financial planning is complicated in many ways, so if you have the option, it makes sense to choose simple over complex

Below we define what we mean by cash, bonds, and stocks. While we discuss individual types of securities here, it's important to remember that we aren't advocating a single type, but rather a well-diversified portfolio.

Cash (and Equivalents)

Cash and its equivalents are short-term, liquid investments that carry little to no volatility. Examples include:

- Savings accounts
- Short-term government treasury bills
- Banker's acceptance paper
- Money market mutual funds

There are many options in the short-term paper market that will provide you with long and well-documented track records, and often government guarantees are available. These are considered by many to be risk free—their standard deviation (see chapter 6) is virtually zero. However, it's important to remember that no investment is able to protect you from all risks. While these investments provide excellent safety for your capital, they don't protect you from the effects of inflation or income tax.

We consider these investments very suitable for a mindful portfolio, provided you take the time to understand their limitations and the rates and fees associated with them.

Bonds (Fixed Income)

Bonds are issued by both companies and governments, and represent a loan made to the issuer by an investor. In return for providing the loan, investors receive fixed interest payments at predetermined intervals until the maturity date of the bond. Upon maturity, the full face value of the bond is repaid to the investor.

Bond rating agencies estimate the level of risk that a particular bond carries. The calculation of risk relates to the ability of the issuer to make the interest payments and repay the loan at maturity. Although rating agencies have recently come under a great deal of fire, they are still a common and useful tool for investors to use when judging the fairness of the interest rate in relation to the level of risk. Interest rates are also determined based on the length of time the investor has to wait to be repaid his principal and what comparable securities are paying at the time of issue.

You should be aware of three facts when considering bonds for your portfolio:

1. If you hold your bond to maturity, you'll be repaid its full face value. However, if you need to sell your bond prior to maturity, you'll likely not receive the same amount you invested, nor will you pay face value if you buy a bond when it's trading on the market after its initial issue. Consider that when interest rates rise, the value of your

bond falls (new bonds issued will pay a buyer a higher interest rate than yours will), and when interest rates fall, the value of your bond rises (new bonds issued will pay a buyer a lower interest rate than yours will).

2. Risk rating changes alter the price of bonds.

3. The longer the term of the bond (the farther away the maturity date is), the greater the effect of (1) and (2) on the price of the bond. Therefore, longer-term bonds are considered to have more price volatility than shorter-term ones.

The pricing of bonds is not as transparent as the pricing of a stock, making it difficult for individuals to trade them on their own. Most investors use a broker or money manager to buy, sell, and manage their bonds.

As long as you're comfortable with the pricing fluctuations of bonds, they make a suitable addition to a mindful portfolio.

Stocks

The word "stocks" often makes people nervous, but stocks, in and of themselves, are neither good nor bad. Stocks (or shares) simply represent ownership in a company. When a public company needs money to expand, or a private company needs to create liquidity, it issues shares to indicate that the owner of these shares has invested in the company. These shares are bought and sold on a stock market.

Well-chosen, good quality stocks can offer value to every kind of investor, large and small. Consider that managers entrusted with investing large pools of money, such as pension fund managers, utilize balanced portfolios containing cash, bonds, and, yes, stocks. With such a large responsibility, why would they veer away from the safety of bonds and guaranteed investments? Because they're trying to achieve a balance between safety and return. In addition to protecting their capital they also must generate some measure of capital gains in order to keep pace with the cost of living. The same applies to the individual investor.

When we refer to stocks in terms of a financial plan we refer to large diversified portfolios, not a single holding. When they are held in this form, you can usually find a track record that will give you a historical rate of return or a benchmark that you can use to estimate the future standard deviation. Therefore, for the purposes of creating a mindful portfolio, stocks are considered suitable.

Selecting Investment Products

The three core investments can be purchased in many different forms, and when considering how to create a portfolio of investments you need to think about what vehicles or investment products you would like to use. Depending on your individual circumstances you can use a single method or a combination of any or all of these. Each of the basic forms of investment—cash, stocks, and bonds—can be purchased using the following suggested methods.

Investment Method	Benefits	Drawbacks
Individual securities	• Fairly low cost if you use a buy-and-hold strategy • Mental stimulation • Frequent contact with your broker and/or portfolio	• Possible lack of diversification • Home bias (bias toward stocks from your local geographic area) • Lack of knowledge/ methodology • Losing interest
Mutual funds	• Instant diversification • Professional management • Easy-to-understand track record of performance • Good statements and tax reporting	• Some have high management fees • Loss of clarity (complicated diver-sification strategies may make it difficult to know where you stand at a given point in time) • Can be inefficient from a tax standpoint
Index funds or exchange-traded funds (ETFs)	• Low management cost • Easy to diversify	• Lack of clarity because of too many competing choices • Often more volatile than comparable mutual funds (because of lack of a cash com-ponent to act as a buffer)

continued on page 114

continued from page 113

Investment Method	Benefits	Drawbacks
		• Trading fees on cash flow in or out can mount up
A portfolio of separately managed accounts (individual securities that are owned by the client but bundled into a professionally managed portfolio; usually purchased through a broker.*) * except for very high-net-worth individuals who can deal directly with money managers	• Tax efficiency • Costs and fees are transparent and, on larger accounts, often lower than comparable mutual fund fees • Ongoing due diligence by the brokerage firm that hires the managers* • Good, easy-to-understand reporting * unless you deal directly with the manager	• High minimum levels of investment (anywhere from $100,000 and up per account)

If you used an investment advisor to help you construct your financial plan (see chapter 6) and design your Investment Policy Statement (IPS) (see chapter 8), this individual will undoubtedly have a preference or bias for one of these methods of investing, and will try to steer you toward it. It would be a mistake for both of you to simply follow that path without consideration. The best way to decide which route to take is to take a step back.

First of all, review the description of each vehicle and combine it with your current investment knowledge and biases. Some biases that will affect your decision include:

- You know you will be annoyed about paying fees.
- You lack confidence in your own financial decisions.
- You've had bad experiences trusting people in the past.
- You like to work as part of a team.
- You prefer to work on your own.

Second, use the mindful decision–making algorithm to help clarify your decision (you'll find a full description in appendix A). Essentially it goes as follows:

1. Clearly define the decision you want to consider in the Talk, Image, and Feel spaces.

2. Actively consider the decision in all three spaces.

3. Passively inquire into the three spaces.

Diversification

As we all know, higher returns also often entail higher risk or volatility. This can create a dangerous situation in which you are withdrawing money at low points or investing at high points. Fortunately, it's possible to reduce the risk of this happening by diversifying your portfolio through asset allocation.

Securities are either positively or negatively correlated to each other. When two securities, or markets, move closely in concert with each other, this is positive correlation; when they move in opposite directions it's known as negative correlation. Modern Portfolio Theory promotes the idea that diversifying between stocks, bonds, and cash (which are negatively correlated) allows investors to mitigate some of the risk in their portfolios, while sacrificing none of the return on the individual securities. Allocating your assets in this way is considered to be the only "free lunch" in the investment world, because it doesn't cost you any extra to structure your portfolio in this manner.

Rather than fleeing to the safety of cash or bonds when the market is bad, or adding extra equities to your portfolio when the market is running up, picking an asset allocation mix that works for your particular circumstances and goals is more sensible. Periodically rebalance the portfolio to bring it back in line with your original allocation. For example, if the equities market has been particularly strong, you'll need to sell off some of your holdings to bring your percentage of stock investments back to target. Keep in mind that periodic, measured rebalancing is not the same thing as panicking and selling at a low or buying at a high.

Hindsight is always 20/20 and investors often bemoan losses (or lost opportunities) and point the finger at their brokers or equity managers. They seem to think that the managers should have intuited that the market was going to move one way or another (after all, they're paying for his or her advice, right?). Unfortunately, this doesn't happen, firstly because very few managers are prescient, and secondly because if they were, it would make constructing a portfolio to meet specific goals impossible—you'd never be able to reliably know what you were invested in, day to day. Imagine that you have a portfolio run by five different managers, two investing in bonds and three in equities, with an approximate split of 40% bonds and 60% equities. Your aim is to generate a yield of 5%–6% per annum. The equity managers suddenly wake up one morning convinced that the markets are going to crash and they liquidate their stock holdings. Now you have a portfolio that's gone from 40% bonds and 60% equities to 40% bonds and 60% cash. In this scenario, two things can happen:

1. The managers are right, but you're in trouble anyway. While your capital has been preserved for the time being, how will you trust the manager to reinvest your cash at the right time? Plus there's no guarantee that this sort of shift will work in the future. You'll have difficulty achieving peace of mind because you'll never be quite sure what you're invested in at any given time.

   OR

2. The managers are wrong, and the market continues to soar while you sit in cash. It's very difficult to re-enter the market, especially when (a) it's rising and (b) you've panicked and exited in fear. Now you'll suffer from both regret and loss of peace of mind.

(Note that while we're using managers in this example, this scenario is just as likely, if not more so, to happen to individual investors.)

It's important to stick to the fundamentals. If your original portfolio mix is suitable for your needs and the managers maintain their style and stick to their mandate, you should be able to survive the market's numerous movements. While rebalancing is important as your portfolio drifts away from the desired percentages, it's important to do so in a considered way. The above example of a macro shift represents movement away from the desired asset allocation, rather than a measured, appropriate move back toward it.

STRUCTURING YOUR PORTFOLIO

There are many different ways to put together a portfolio. To help you get started, here are two simple examples—the core and explore method and the balanced portfolio method.

Core and Explore

The idea here is to build a core portfolio that you periodically rebalance back to the original mix. Approximately 80%–90% of your portfolio should be invested in the core. The remainder can be used to invest in whatever strikes your fancy at the time. This slush fund of explore money is there as a safety valve to keep you interested without tinkering with the main portfolio.

The core and explore method is a good idea for advisors and clients who feel the need to satiate the "I must have the next big thing" feeling as it prevents them from feeling left out. There is one problem, though—you can often lose track of these odd investments and even forget that you own them. It's a little like what can happen at the grocery store; you carefully build your core basket of fruits, vegetables, and other sensible foods, but keep back a small portion of the food basket for all the exciting stuff they put at the checkouts. Months later you notice a can of organic chestnuts in the back of the pantry and wonder what you were thinking when you bought them. Imagine how much worse it is when you're looking at your portfolio statement and find some strange structured investment or a single stock that you remember nothing about.

Advisors often aren't fans of this method. It's difficult for us to have myriad tiny client positions. There's liability if we fail to monitor them on an ongoing basis, and often the minimum commissions charged by the firm on the small trades bite too deeply into any potential client profits. However, if the advisor or client has a particular interest or knowledge in a specific area, such as gold, silver, or real estate investment trusts, the core and explore method can be a useful way to exploit this knowledge. ETFs are a particularly good way to buy these investments. If this isn't the case for you and you want to follow the core and explore method to dabble in small positions, we recommend that, unless your advisor has an interest in small positions, you use a discount brokerage for the explore portion of the portfolio.

Balanced Portfolio

Generally speaking, traditional balanced portfolios follow a weighting of 60% stocks and 40% fixed income. Historically this has been a sound strategy for long-term income and growth; however, there is flexibility. For example, more conservative investors may choose to reverse the order and go with 40% stocks and 60% fixed income, while younger, more aggressive investors may find 80% stocks and 20% fixed income is a more suitable mix.

Often advisors will use age as a guide to determine the weighting; in fact, some mutual fund companies have portfolios that adjust the mix based on your age, lessening the equity weighting as the portfolio (and investor) matures. Investors sometimes think that because they are retired they shouldn't have any equity component in their mix. They're mistaken though, because according to life expectancy tables, a person retiring at age 65 can expect to live between another 15 and 25 years. That's a fairly long time horizon. You can reduce your risk by carefully considering both your long- and short-term goals. While you don't want to be cavalier, you must take some steps to ensure that your capital doesn't run out before you do.

As a mindful investor, you'll want to set your original portfolio mix in conjunction with your advisor and base the decision on your own overall situation. Both your advisor and your financial planning software will have useful tools to help you determine the optimal mix.

When you have settled on a portfolio that feels comfortable for you, return to your financial plan and enter the percentage or dollar values of each component you've chosen and add the standard deviations of each component. Then update the Monte Carlo simulation graph (chapter 6). Are you satisfied with the projections or do they make you lose confidence? If you're not happy with them, then you or your planner should adjust the weightings until you are both comfortable. While only an indicator, this simulation is the closest preview you'll get of the real thing. And remember, you're not trying to win at some great investment game, you're simply looking for a portfolio that you're comfortable with—one that allows you to meet your long-term goals and still maintain clarity, equanimity, and peace of mind.

MANAGEMENT STYLE

There are two major schools of thought in the investment world, and debate rages between them over whether portfolios should be actively or passively managed. Active managers believe that investors can find stocks and markets that are mispriced relative to their current value, usually because of euphoria and pessimism, and that good managers and clever investors can beat the market averages over a long period of time. Conversely, followers of the Efficient Market Hypothesis (EMH) believe that access to the same pool of knowledge is readily available at all times to all investors, and this makes it impossible to beat the market as a whole. They believe that the only way to get a higher return is to assume more risk.

Active Investing

Value is one of the most common forms of active investing. Benjamin Graham is considered to be the father of value investing, and Warren Buffett is a keen follower of his investment philosophy. Benjamin Graham's favourite allegory is of Mr. Market, a character who turns up every day at a shareholder's door offering to buy or sell his shares at a differing price. Often Mr. Market quotes a price that seems plausible, but sometimes it seems ridiculous. The shareholder can agree to the suggested price and trade with him, or ignore him; Mr. Market won't mind, he'll be back again tomorrow. The point of the story is that investors shouldn't regard the whims of the market as a determining factor in the value of their shares. Mindful investors who follow the value style concentrate on the real-life performance of companies and the dividends they pay to investors, rather than being overly concerned with Mr. Market's often irrational behaviour.

Value managers are considered to be active investors, and set target prices for buying and selling based on fundamental analysis of what they believe to be the value of a company. This value analysis is related to the manager's own criteria for overvalue or undervalue. It could be based on one or all of the following factors: price-to-book value, high dividend yield, low price-earnings ratio, or the intrinsic value calculation (summing future income generated and discounting it to present value).

Other active investment styles include:

- Growth: a portfolio of companies whose earnings are expected to rise

- Momentum: securities are purchased with the belief that their current movement (either up or down) will continue

- Economic Value Added (EVA): companies are valued on net operating profit minus cost of capital

- Technical Analysis: a variety of investment methods that are based on tracking pattern changes in the price and volume of securities, often using charting techniques

- Small cap: companies with a relatively small market capitalization

- Growth at a reasonable price (GARP): a blend of selected growth stocks with some value criteria added

Passive Investing

Exchange-traded funds (ETFs) or index funds are the favoured investment of EMH managers and investors. Each unit represents a share in an overall index and the fund's performance tracks the performance of the underlying index. ETFs are now astoundingly diverse; you can find one that covers almost any style index, market index, or commodity index. In fact, if an index or market of any kind exists, you can find an ETF that matches it.

ETFs are attractive because they are available without the same level of management fees incurred by mutual funds and managed portfolios, but remember that ETFs are bought and sold with trading commissions. These commissions can quickly mount up if you are making regular additions or withdrawals and trading the portfolio. Also, the often onerous administration and ongoing tax reporting of these trades, plus the tracking of dividends and interest, are the responsibility of the investor.

If an advisor is helping to manage your ETFs, they'll often offer you the option of "wrapping" them in a fee-based account. This fee will add an expense to the portfolio that is often equal to managed account or mutual fund annual fees.

So which way do we lean in this active versus passive debate? Toward the mindful one of course; that is, the one that *you* feel most confident with. Remember, it's your portfolio and you have to believe in it. It's important to keep in mind that you can easily combine the two styles.

DUE DILIGENCE

Whichever methods you select, you, your advisor, and/or his firm must conduct due diligence to ensure that your investments continue to be suitable and are avoiding style drift (that is, they are being managed in the same way as when you originally selected them). If you're using a separately managed portfolio, your advisor's firm will conduct the due diligence reviews as part of their service. They'll check to ensure that the managers are performing well in relation to an appropriate benchmark, and are following their particular process (over time there can be a style drift as the portfolio shifts away from the original model; it's important that it's rebalanced appropriately to reflect changes in both the market and the securities so that you can be confident that the investment will still meet your goals). They'll also keep an eye out for changes in the manager's organization (such as loss of key personnel), unexpected performance figures, or changes in investment philosophy. While these things may be innocuous and simply the normal course of business, being aware of them and proactive in addressing them can assist in the prevention of performance issues.

While your advisor's firm has the advantage of size, a team of professionals, and connections to help it obtain any necessary information, you too can and should conduct due diligence if you manage your own portfolio of stocks or mutual funds. Here are some questions to get you started:

- Are you regularly rebalancing your portfolio so that it still reflects your original asset allocation?

- Are your positions trading with enough volume for you to easily exit them if necessary, without a large difference between the bid price and the ask price?

- Do you have adequate research tools?

- Can you benchmark your portfolio against an index to give you an idea of how you are fairing?

- Do you hold onto any positions for illogical reasons (attachment), such as "I'll just wait until it gets back to what I paid for it, then I'll sell"?

- Are you confident enough in your portfolio that you could run your mother's portfolio? Can you explain your process to her?

- The fee you pay yourself is equivalent to what you save by not employing a professional manager. Are you worth that fee? Could you make more money doing something else?

- When things turn sour, are you able to remain equanimous with a balanced state of calm and focus, enabling you to make sound decisions?

FINAL THOUGHTS

Here are some final thoughts on portfolio construction:

- Maintaining a beginner's mind is key. Make sure to keep asking lots of questions, even if you've already asked and think you know the answer. As you advance your thinking, you may hear something new or different when you ask again.

- More choices will not necessarily make you happier. Thousands of investments exist, and there's no right answer about which ones are the best at any given time. If you try to diversify too widely, you'll lose track of where you stand.

- The person who tells you they were fully invested in cash and bonds during the market crash was almost certainly telling someone else that they were fully invested in stocks while the market was running up. Neither one is true.

- It's a good idea to periodically translate percentage returns into dollar values for a reality check. If your advisor asks you if you'd be comfortable with a 10% decline, you might well say yes, until you realize that on a $1,000,000 portfolio that translates into $100,000.

- Remember that everything is impermanent, and changing moment by moment. This will help you to maintain perspective, even when you think you've made a bad decision. Simply correct your course of action at the next opportunity, and move on.

Chapter 8

Client/Advisor Relations

The relationship between a client and an advisor has only one ultimate goal: to create financial success for both of you. A successful relationship takes on a life of its own, leading to greater trust, competence, and interest. Every move seems to propel you both forward. Together you can be much more successful than you would be individually. If you have any doubts, just take a look at what happens to unsuccessful relationships. As you likely already know, they quickly come to a stage where every move makes things worse. If like most people you've experienced the negative side of a relationship, you know it's now time to be mindful about your goals and what help you will need to achieve them so you can focus on creating a positive relationship that will work for you.

We like to think of the client/advisor relationship as a mini strategic alliance. Drawing on Maria's years of experience creating large corporate alliances, we'll demonstrate how the same principles and process can be applied here to select an advisor or improve relations between you and your existing advisor. Ideally the advisor you choose will be proficient in areas where you are weak, filling in any potential gaps and making your financial life stronger. You'll need to ensure that you and your advisor are strategically aligned and compatible, so that you can work in harmony toward the same goals.

STRATEGIC ALIGNMENT

Strategic alliances are key to the success of many companies and choosing the right partner is critical to the success of any alliance. As we demonstrate in this overview, many of the same strategies can be applied to your relationship with your advisor.

Creating a successful corporate strategic alliance involves a five-step process that is equally applicable to creating a successful alliance with a financial advisor.

1. *Develop a strategy.* You need to know what your goals are and what you're looking for in your relationship with an advisor before you can find one who suits those needs. If you don't have your own strategy, you'll end up following someone else's, which will make it difficult for you to succeed.

2. *Select an advisor.* Take the time to ensure you select someone who understands and values your strategy, and with whom you're compatible. Many people focus too much on the financial aspects of the deal (for example, fees charged), when that should be secondary. Without understanding and alignment between client and advisor, the relationship will be doomed to failure.

3. *Structure the alliance*. Once you've found an advisor you'd like to work with, it's time to get down to the details. You'll need to work together to decide how the partnership will go forward, including an action plan, responsibilities, fees, et cetera.

4. *Maintain the alliance*. Your relationship with your advisor is just that—a relationship. It requires ongoing maintenance in order to be successful. Both client and advisor need to ensure that the action plan is being carried out properly, and that goals are still in alignment and being met.

5. *Evaluate the alliance*. In addition to performance tracking, periodic reviews are also necessary to make certain that the relationship is still working for both parties. It's important not just to focus on the numbers. Keep in mind that lack of trust and miscommunication also contribute to the failure of alliances.

As with all relationships, some alliances do fail. Here are some of the common pitfalls that can lead to failure:

- Not having a strategy. Without a well-considered strategy and clear goals, it's impossible to measure success.

- Not developing clear expectations. Establishing roles at the outset allows both parties to know what's expected of them and what they can expect from each other.

- Focusing too much on the financial aspect of the alliance (fees incurred). This may lead to neglecting the importance of implementation and success.

- Lack of ongoing commitment. When either party loses interest or feels their needs aren't being met, success can be compromised.

- Lack of meaningful reporting. Make sure that you are both using the same metrics to evaluate the relationship. If one of you expects short-term results, while the other is focused on the long term, someone is going to be disappointed.[1]

EVALUATION

The first step in creating a positive strategic client/advisor relationship is to examine your current situation. At this point, you'll either be working with an advisor or on your own. To evaluate if this method is working for you, honestly answer the following questions:

- Do I have confidence in my/our strategy?

- Do I have trust (usually developed over time)?

- Do I/we have sufficient knowledge?

- Do I/we have sufficient resources?

- Do I feel in control?

If the answer to all of the above is "yes," then congratulations, you're already in a situation that works well for you. If, however, some of the answers are "no," you should think about making changes to make your situation better serve your needs.

There are a few other questions you should consider as you contemplate your relationship with your advisor. In other chapters we have talked about the mindful decision-making process (see appendix A), so if you don't have immediate answers to these questions, then here's a great opportunity to test out the process. Remember to tackle one question at a time with this process.

Advisor-Related Questions

- If you don't have an advisor, ask: Should I have an advisor?
- If you have an advisor, ask: Can I go it alone?
- If you have an advisor, ask: Should I look at changing advisors?

Portfolio-Related Questions

- Am I satisfied with my current risk level?
- Is there a clear investment strategy/methodology?
- Do I need to look at lower-cost alternatives?

The sections below will provide some tips on how to find and develop a better relationship with your advisor, be it your existing one or a new one.

THE RELATIONSHIP PROCESS

There are three main stages in the life of the client/advisor relationship, which are all subsets of the strategic alliance process:

1. The introductory meeting(s) during which you select your advisor.

2. The formal agreement during which you structure the alliance.

3. Ongoing maintenance during which you maintain and evaluate the alliance.

The Introductory Meeting(s)

In reality this may be a series of meetings. Personally, the bulk of my clients first met and assessed me as I conducted workshops on financial planning and money management. If you're looking for an advisor, this is a great way to start checking them out. You can sit back and learn not only about the advisor's products and ideas but also her reactions to other people.

Focus on Sight and Sound during the presentation. Listening to the tone the advisor uses can give you many clues about what kind of person they might be to work with. Focusing on Sight and Sound means you are listening mindfully. Concentrating on sight helps you to read information about body language and facial expressions, and concentrating on Sound allows you to hear what's actually being said, rather than what you think is being said or expect to be said. People who aren't listening mindfully often fall into the trap of only half listening because they're focused on thinking about what they're going to say next, rather than on the message that the speaker's trying to convey. By concentrating on the content and how it's said, you'll have a clearer understanding of the message.

Really you're employing an abbreviated version of the External Awareness method (chapter 3). Try your best to remain in the present moment. Failing to listen properly means you'll miss what's being communicated and, even worse, you'll likely make up what you think must have been said. Being in the present moment is a good habit to get into, because not only will you get more out of your meeting, you'll find it's more relaxing.

When there's a break in the meeting, think about what you've picked up so far. Was the person believable? Are they someone you wish to work with? Are they a mindful listener? Take the time to tune in to internal awareness. What are you experiencing in the Feel, Image, and Talk spaces? Because you've truly listened, you're better able to pay attention to the responses that the discussions have elicited from you. You'll be able to make decisions from a place of clarity and equanimity. If you notice that the advisor's not a mindful listener, beware. If an advisor isn't listening before you become a client, she certainly won't listen once you've signed up. This would result in you feeling like a lesser part of the alliance because your input wasn't being heard, which would eventually make you mistrustful. Consider whether you feel that she has your best interests at heart. Do you feel that the advisor is trying to control you or to empower you? Do you feel like you could learn from this person? Do you sense that she wants you to be successful and that she truly wants this to be a win–win relationship? If not, it won't be sustainable.

You might find this process mechanical in the beginning, but it will become automatic over time. Your judgment will be enhanced and you'll make decisions more easily, efficiently, and effectively. When you're truly present and listening mindfully, meetings are more productive and take less time, freeing you up to do things you enjoy.

My own preference is to find someone who's gentle and relaxed, and seems to have a genuine desire to help. Remember, you're not looking for a tough litigation lawyer or the smartest, most arrogant money manager. At this stage you're looking for someone who's obviously intelligent and who can help you relax enough to talk about your greatest hopes and fears.

During the first personal meeting in the advisor's office you need to assess the advisor's mindset and inclinations. Ideally, you're looking for someone who:

- Sees and respects people fully for what they are. Look carefully at how he treats his staff and how they respond to him. Listen to the tone of the receptionist when she calls to let him know you're waiting.

- Has a real desire to be of service. He probes gently and is completely interested and focused on your greatest hopes and fears. He gives examples of how he's helped other people with the same types of issues, and you're confident that he understands you.

- Has a win-win attitude, where he genuinely seems to think you can both benefit from working together. There's a lot of lip service paid to this, so make sure you find him believable. If the advisor doesn't bring it up, ask him to articulate his thoughts on win-win relationships; his tone and body language will give you lots of information. Trust your gut—what's it telling you? By tuning in to your Feel, Image, and Talk spaces, you'll gain valuable information.

- Has a real depth of knowledge. In particular ask about recent educational experience. It's critical that your advisor continually strives to hone his skills through courses, programs, and designations. It's easy to become stale without continuing education. Also ask what financial books he's read recently.

- Has a *big mind*. That is, a broad perspective. Can he talk about investment methodologies other than his own, or even about other advisors, in a tolerant, stable, and impartial manner?

- Works wholeheartedly for every client that he takes on, without discrimination over account size. Remember, if he has relative judgment based on account size, you may one day find yourself relegated to the unattractive status of a minor client. Most advisors now are clear and up front about the minimum account size that they work with. There may be other members on their team who work with smaller accounts. If this is the case, and you don't meet the minimum requirement, then your meeting should be with the other team member.

When you listen mindfully, you'll be able to tell if the person is genuine and forthright. Make sure that you don't let your own insecurities and fears get in the way. This takes practice, but with time you'll be able to distinguish between your own interference and what you're picking up externally. Does the advisor look you directly in the eye or does he shift away in discomfort when he's telling you something? Does he try to change your mind, ignoring what you've said and focusing on convincing you that he's correct? These all provide clear messages about the character of the advisor. Remember that you're trying to establish an alliance, which is a relationship—you have to feel comfortable and happy in it. You shouldn't marry someone expecting that you can change them, and the same holds true for this relationship. You can't fix what you don't like about your advisor, and in fact, anything you don't like now will only be magnified over the course of the alliance, particularly in stressful times.

The Formal Agreement

Before you actually start working with an advisor, it's recommended that you draft a formal agreement between the two of you. These agreements are usually called Investment Policy Statements (IPSs). Most cover the following main areas:

- Description of client
- Time horizon for money to be invested
- Risk tolerance
- Approved investments
- Cash flow requirements
- Portfolio structure
- Standard deviation
- Review process (written reports, and quarterly, semi-annual, or annual meetings)

While IPSs are a good beginning, we don't think that they go far enough. They are usually boilerplate rather than customized, and questionnaire based, which can result in you being pigeonholed into one of a number of set categories. Standard structure and wording is adapted from documents usually used with pension funds. This means they can be wordy and difficult to understand.

We recommend that you go a step further and incorporate some of the key Mindfulness principles into your version.

Review the IPS with your advisor and ask him or her to adjust it so that rather than outlining a "recipient/provider of service" relationship like a typical IPS does, yours will represent a mini strategic alliance between you and your advisor. Ensure that he or she incorporates:

- The strategy and expectations for your working relationship together (including an action plan, detailed responsibilities for you and the team members, and fees to be charged)

- Details regarding meaningful reporting, so that you all are using the same set of criteria to evaluate whether or not the relationship is working

- Plans to educate and empower you

- A financial plan

- Methods for ongoing communication and for determining when meetings will be beneficial

Ongoing Maintenance

In addition to account monitoring and assisting with due diligence, advisors should endeavour to educate their clients, alert them to new ideas, and give them any information that may be useful in clarifying and empowering the relationship. Continuing education isn't just important for the advisor, but also for the client. In this mindful process, it's important that the advisor, his team, and his firm continually strive to empower the client. The advisor does this by determining gaps in the client's knowledge and understanding, and by educating the client to fill these knowledge gaps.

It's also critical that the team has a goal to empower the client to be familiar with their portfolio and the decisions that are made about it. Clear client statements and online access assist with this process, and can prompt interesting discussions. Clients must never be made to feel stupid when asking questions about their accounts, but should be encouraged to ask for clarification at every stage. The reasons for this are threefold:

1. A client should never stay with an advisor because of dependence. It's a weak relationship that can never harness synergy between the two parties.

2. It avoids a relationship where the advisor can win at the client's expense.

3. People negotiate better and can move forward more confidently when they feel secure in their level of knowledge. If the advisor takes the time to educate her clients now, when she comes up with a great idea in the future, the clients will be able to quickly take advantage of it.

Remember there are no stupid questions. Be sure to ask all questions that occur to you. It's the advisor's responsibility to answer all of them, no matter how simple or complex.

It's also important to remember that while the advisor acts as a coach and a guide for the client, as the client you'll be expected to take ownership of the decisions that are made regarding your portfolio. At the end of the day, responsibility for your money rests squarely on your shoulders. You need to take the counsel and information provided by your advisor and make sure that the decisions made are truly the right ones for you. In addition to regularly evaluating your portfolio, you should also be evaluating the alliance to ensure that you're continuing to benefit from it and that it's helping you to achieve your goals. This stage in the alliance process is about exerting control where you can. From a place of equanimity and calm acceptance of what you are experiencing, make any required changes or simply affirm your satisfaction with the present state of the relationship. Make sure it's a conscious and deliberate process.

HALLMARKS OF A WELL-RUN PRACTICE

Once you've found an advisor with whom you think you'd like to work, take the time to see how he runs his practice. Both clients and advisors benefit when an advisor runs a smooth, efficient business. Here are 10 indicators that an advisor has taken the time to consider how best to empower clients and to improve service levels. He or she:

1. Creates a financial plan for you—or has one created for you

2. Writes either an IPS or a mindful policy statement

3. Provides and encourages the use of online account access; if the client statements prepared by the firm lack clarity, the advisor teaches you how to read and understand them

4. Schedules regular meetings that aren't based on a formula, but rather with the idea that together you work out a natural rhythm based on need (online access has taken away a lot of the need for regular meetings)

5. Educates you in every meeting or call, particularly if there's an area that he or she is enthusiastic about, or where recent news items may have raised questions

6. Is skeptical; both advisor and client have to winnow out the facts of schemes that purport to be a new way of doing something

7. Returns calls as quickly as possible

8. Encourages clients to call the team member responsible for addressing the need that exists at any particular time—it's inefficient to call an advisor with a simple administrative question or an assistant with a question regarding overall portfolio strategy

9. After a major market correction, takes the time to assess your reaction—you both may be surprised by how calm or frightened you were and talking to your advisor about these reactions may help you to decide whether or not you need to adjust the risk level of the portfolio

10. Pushes you to create a budget, because it can save your financial life

You may find that your existing relationship lacks in some of the areas. If you're a client and this bothers you, don't be passive and allow resentment to build. Instead, help your advisor to help you by explaining the areas you would like to see expanded, improved, or changed. If you're an advisor and would like to re-energize your practice, or be more competitive or more proactive, then begin to implement any necessary changes you've learned you need to make.

Treating your client/advisor relationship like a strategic alliance is a good way to maximize the success of the relationship. Creating a mindful relationship and treating it like a business is smart. It can help you deal productively with the emotion that often surrounds finances. You'll be able to evaluate your situation more objectively and make better decisions about the partnership.

Chapter 9

When Things Go Wrong

Despite all of your goal setting, planning, and hoping, things can, and do, go wrong. Many things can derail your financial future if you don't handle them properly, including illness, death, divorce or separation, job loss, debt, business failure, stock market correction, and fraud and scams. Each of these on its own could fill a book, but we'll lightly address them here and offer suggestions for ways that you can deal with them so that their impact on you and your financial future is minimized.

There are many resources at your disposal to help you evaluate and improve your situation when one of these disasters strikes. For instance, your planner can show you a new forecast, review some options with you, and perhaps add some perspective to your situation; your accountant may be able to show you how to mitigate the damage through tax relief; and your lawyer may be able to help you with the legal issues that arise. However, you must understand that in order to regain stability in your life following a major financial disruption, you'll first need to deal with the pain and suffering it's caused. You must face the problem head on and not wait around, hoping in vain that someone else will take the pain away.

It's important to remember that everyone in the world will be affected by at least some of these "disruptive" events at some point during their life. Often when you experience loss or pain, the immediate feeling is one of solitude and it's as if you're the only person who's ever experienced this problem or the only one who's ever made such a big mistake. This feeling is dangerous because it tends to lead to despair. Be aware that others all over the world are suffering in your current situation too. Develop a habit of thinking of the pain of others and wishing them well. This may seem strange at first, but as you practise having compassion for others, you'll find you also develop it for yourself. This can help to prevent you from beating yourself up when you feel you have made mistakes.

It's also important to remember that the anguish, fear, sadness, anger, guilt, and despair that accompany life's challenges and tragedies are absolutely normal. Experiencing these emotions simply means that you're human. You need to be able to embrace them all and to accept them with equanimity if you are going to heal (remember, this means allowing the emotions to arise naturally, without interfering with or resisting them). You can't prevent yourself from experiencing these emotions in your life, but you can apply a technique that will allow you to experience them fully so you can prevent the suffering that comes from resistance and suppression. This will allow you to experience purification and freedom from the tyranny of your mind. As Shinzen Young said, "In life, pain is unavoidable but suffering is optional."

When a serious challenge arises, unless your immediate action will save the day or prevent a tragedy, we suggest that the best strategy is to do nothing until you have regained your composure and can be in the present moment. By widening the gap between stimulus and response, you'll be able to see more clearly and make better decisions. The wider the gap, the better the decisions.

While this sounds good in theory, how do you actually do it? Begin by working with the Internal Awareness technique described in chapter 3. When unpleasant things arise at the same time in the Feel, Image, and Talk spaces, it's easy to become overwhelmed and spiral out of control. Try to divide and conquer—become aware of each space separately. When you do this, you'll be better able to untangle the feelings and thoughts, and to gain control of your mind. Of course, this will take practice, but you'll quickly benefit.

Take the time to do a formal meditation. Make contact with your Feel centres, the mental screen in front of or behind your eyes, and place awareness at the ears or around the head where you experience Talk. Now, in a rhythmic way, start to note what's arising in these spaces. If Feel, Image, and Talk are all arising at the same time, just pick one to focus on, and then notice what arises a few seconds later. You'll realize that over time doing this will bring some relief and, eventually, peace, even with very difficult experiences. Don't despair if it doesn't happen immediately; be persistent and patient. No matter how difficult it may be to execute the technique at first, remember that the alternative is being controlled relentlessly by your mind.

If you find that the intensity of what you're experiencing is too great and that you can't bear to become internally aware at this moment, work instead with the External Awareness technique in your formal meditation. Working with Touch, Sight, and Sound or a subset of these enables you to focus your attention externally. You may experience relief with this technique as it brings you into the present moment. Bringing yourself to the present moment makes you aware that there is only this moment, and that moment by moment you can handle life's challenges.

Generally you can bear just one moment at a time; bringing too many moments together in the form of the future can introduce worry and fear into the mind. Maintaining your focus on the present moment prevents you from creating suffering. Most of us can usually handle pain, even great pain, but when we introduce resistance (and therefore suffering) we may be overwhelmed and become fearful that we can't cope.

Above all, remember to be very gentle and patient with yourself. As human beings we're both tremendously resilient and fragile. With a little gentleness we can cope much more readily. As difficult as it may be to believe, it's often these very painful moments that provide the greatest refinement of consciousness and personal growth and with that, potentially deep inner peace.

ILLNESS

Illness can take many forms and affect your finances in many ways, whether through medical costs, in-home health care costs, lost income due to time off work, forced retirement, and so on. Your advisor can help you determine what kind of impact this will have on your short- and long-term finances. Any of the above can be broken down into approximate dollar values and entered into your financial plan. If you're lucky, your plan will be strong enough to withstand the change in circumstance without affecting your goals. If not, you'll have to start making decisions. This is always tough when you don't feel well or you are worried about someone close to you who is ill. Take the time to calm yourself with the techniques above.

DEATH

We'll cover planning for your death in more detail in chapter 10. If you're the survivor in this situation, the most important thing is simply to make sure that you're financially safe for enough time as it will take for your wounds to heal. If at all avoidable, you shouldn't make any major financial decisions until you have become accustomed to your new situation and are feeling strong and confident enough to make good decisions.

DIVORCE OR SEPARATION

The financial consequences of divorce or separation are greatly underestimated. If you're getting divorced or separated, our advice here is simple—reduce your expectations for the future. When you were married you might have had a nice house in a good neighbourhood. Now you may end up renting a nice apartment instead. Same goes for the cottage. Use your financial plan to determine the outcome of several different scenarios; this can definitely help frame the questions you need to ask yourself. Even if you feel that you're at fault for the divorce, take the time to consider every demand. Make use of the mindful decision-making process (appendix Λ) to help you maintain equanimity while making these tough decisions.

JOB LOSS

Most people will lose a job at some time in their lives, and almost all survive. Again, you should visit your financial advisor and run a variety of scenarios. Once you have the facts and figures you can make better, more informed decisions, such as wait for recall, find another job, or retire early.

DEBT

A little debt, used wisely, can be a good thing. After all, almost no one would be able to afford a house without the help of a mortgage. Here we're referring to seemingly insurmountable consumer debt. As we mentioned in chapter 6, a $5,000 credit card bill can quickly mount up. If you only make the minimum monthly payments (2.5%), you'll be making them for 26 years, and will pay a whopping $7,000 in interest alone.

It's easy to see how things can quickly spiral out of control if you're not prudent with your use of credit.

Being mindful in your daily life should prove very beneficial when it comes to managing a debt problem. Often people fall into credit difficulty because they suffer from attachment; aversion; ignorance, confusion, and delusion; envy and jealousy; and pride—all the hindrances we have been discussing. Being aware of these hindrances and avoiding falling into their trap will help you steer clear of a credit crunch brought on by too much conspicuous consumption. Here are a few other tips for dealing with your debt and maintaining your credit rating:

- Remain current on your bills. It seems obvious, but you must make at least the minimum payment on your bills each month. Failing to do so can affect your credit rating and increase your interest rate.

- Stay informed. Make sure you know your credit score and periodically check your credit report (available from a credit bureau) for errors and possible misuse.

- If you do find that you've accumulated debts along the way, try to consolidate them into one loan. You'll find it easier to manage one payment rather than many smaller ones, and you may be able to negotiate a lower interest rate because the size of the loan will be larger.

- Keep in contact with your lender. If you run into a situation that is out of control and you have to miss a payment (perhaps through illness or a job layoff), don't hide out and hope they won't notice— they will. Instead, contact them and let them know your current circumstances. Ask if they have any solutions or alternatives to offer that will allow them to be repaid while still accommodating your current circumstances. Approaching them early means you'll have more options available to you. If you give in to delusion or ignorance and try to forget about the problem until it balloons, your options will be severely limited.

BUSINESS FAILURE

Approximately 90% of businesses fail within the first two years, so we recommend that you don't enter your business as an asset on your financial plan. Instead, treat it as a job and enter as income the cash flow it pays you. Enter the investment assets it owns (over and above the operating capital) as assets only if you could take them without hurting the company. This prevents you from being financially devastated by the loss of a business.

The only time you would count the business as an asset would be if you were shortly going to sell it and a business valuator had given you a value or you had been receiving offers. At that point it would be prudent to include it in your financial plan, because you'd need to begin making plans for how to invest and protect that capital.

STOCK MARKET CORRECTION

Imagine you open up your account statement and discover that you've lost a third of your life savings. You're bound to be overcome with emotion. Before you do anything, you need to gain control of your mind. It may be helpful to formally prac-tise a relaxation technique we described in chapter 3. Take the time to sit or lie down and focus on your breath. Take slow, even breaths and count to three or four as you breathe in and three or four as you breathe out. Find your own rhythm and do this until you feel that you have calmed down. Alternatively or in addition to the breath practice, you can work with the body relaxation technique, also described in chapter 3. Start with your feet and work your way up to your head, relaxing each body part as you go. You may even wish to work with the Internal Awareness and External Awareness techniques as described earlier in that chapter.

Once you feel calmer and more stable, you'll be better able to listen and make good decisions, ones that aren't based on panic and fear. With any luck the synergy you have created with your advisor (see chapter 8) will allow you both to use skillful means to evaluate and deal with the situation, even if that means doing nothing. Once you have assembled as many facts as pos-sible, you'll need to make a decision, usually "Should I sell my securities now?" Again, the mindful decision-making process (appendix A) can help you determine the right answer for you.

Once you've calmly and carefully examined your situation, you'll need to make a decision that you're comfortable with. Generally speaking, if your plan was designed to comfortably meet your goals and the Monte Carlo simulator indicates you'll be successful, then in the event of catastrophe you should still likely be able to hold on to your investments until things stabilize. Remember that the decision to sell won't be your final decision. At some point you'll have to decide when, and if, to get back into the market. This often can be a difficult, and expensive, decision.

In our sections on planning and diversification we talked about standard deviation and how it helps you to forecast 95% of the market situations in which you could find yourself. Unfortunately, it only applies to 95% of situations, and this means the markets may go beyond that 5% of the time (or, on average, once every 20 years). Without a doubt, this is a time when your equanimity—your ability to accept calmly what is arising in your sensory experience (Feel/Image/Talk) at this very moment—will be tested. If you are being driven to distraction by worry, then go ahead and have your planner put where you stand currently (at or near the bottom) into your financial plan. If the plan shows that it would fail based on these numbers, then you'll need to adjust the spending or the retirement date until it shows some chance of success. At least you'll be making changes based on facts, rather than from a place of fear and supposition, and you'll gain some measure of peace knowing that you're addressing the situation.

FRAUD

Of all the ways to lose money, fraud can be the cruelest. The loss often feels deeper and more personal because it wasn't the result of a random act of market movement or timing; rather, someone intentionally tried to part you from your money. Sometimes the scams can actually involve an underlying threat of violence; they will certainly involve shame and embarrassment. I can speak from experience here. While working as a summer student in a hotel, I met a classic con man. This ancient fellow claimed he was a former personal manservant of a famous knight. Throughout that summer he concocted an elaborate tale of meeting a nurse and wooing her; they planned to get married in the fall. One day he said that he had to make a small deposit for his reception hall or else he would lose his booking. Unfortunately, he had forgotten to go to the bank and needed a small loan from me to tide him over to the next day. I had no problem with this because a couple of weeks before he had "found" my pay envelope on the floor of the locker room (we were paid in cash in those days) and returned it to me. After that I trusted him implicitly and felt great to be able to help him out with a loan (even if it was two-thirds of my pay). Unfortunately, so did the other 12 employees he took advantage of in exactly the same manner. We never saw him or our money again. I think in this case his approach of returning money to gain our trust before going for the big scam was what made his scheme work so well, as he effectively disabled our screening ability. The point of this story is that while we'd like to believe that there are signs that a fraudster gives out, in reality there aren't always.

Ponzi Schemes

These schemes involve taking money from one investor and paying some of it to another in the form of interest or profit. Recently they seem to have had a major resurgence. In reality they've always been around, but many have come to light recently only because a large number of people needed their capital back from these schemes in order to cover legitimate market losses and margin calls. This large withdrawal of capital causes the schemes to collapse; they need a steady inflow of cash in order to pay earlier investors.

The other key to successful Ponzi schemes is their ability to return some, or all, of your early investments with great bonus interest or profit. The con man running the scheme has no trouble paying this to you; he just takes it from the capital his new "investors" have given him. After that, there's no question that in most cases you'll be back for more of this easy money. After all, you now trust this person and view the investment as safe. While the Madoff case, featured in the news in 2009, was unusual in its large size, small to medium-size versions are much more common.

If you think a current investment you are involved with has the feel of a Ponzi scheme, start doing some research. Can you really understand how the profits are being made? Remember our rule about keeping it simple with stocks, bonds, and/or cash. Do the investments fit any of these categories? If so, ask yourself how it possibly could be working out so much better than anything comparable. Without making a fuss, ask to take out your capital. Then, while you are waiting to put it back in (if that's your plan), start making inquiries. In particular have your accountant, lawyer, and other financial advisors review the investments and statements and tell you how they work. If they can't explain it to you and you can't figure it out, you may be wise to give it a pass. When something seems too good to be true, it usually is.

Telemarketing Fraud

When you were a child your parents probably told you not to talk to strangers. Well, I'm about to tell you it all over again. There is nothing—I repeat: *nothing*—that will come to you in the form of a phone call or email from a stranger that will benefit you in any way, shape, or form. Just as (spoiler alert) there's no Easter Bunny or Tooth Fairy, there are no lottery winnings from a game you can't remember playing, no Nigerian money waiting for you in Switzerland, no free vacation. In most of these cases you will be asked to send cash, provide information from your bank account (to deposit your good fortune), or give your credit card number to cover tax or administrative costs. And voila, your cash becomes their cash, your bank account becomes their bank account, and your credit card becomes their credit card.

As a normal human being, you are wired to work within society and to help, trust, and be polite to other people. This built-in trust developed over millions of years, and is required for our society to function. But it also provides an entry point for manipulation experts. Once you have let them in and start speaking to them, they becomes like a virus—almost impossible to get rid of.

If you haven't been conned yet, you just haven't spoken to the right con man. If you've been conned before, the bad news is you may be conned again. No one is immune if the approach is tailored to them. Your immune system is weakened when you are under stress, ill, or in the grip of emotions, and if you pick up the phone or open email in that condition, you may be vulnerable.

PUTTING LOSS INTO PERSPECTIVE

It's important to put loss into perspective. As difficult as it is to consider, everything is impermanent. We repeat: everything is impermanent. All of life is constantly changing, and we'll all experience loss at one time or another. You win some, and you lose some. If you're going through great times, remember that sooner or later these will end, as we witnessed in the market collapse in the fall of 2008. Conversely, if you're going through difficult or even excruciating times, you can find solace in the fact that these too shall pass. Not only will they pass, but in fact they're already passing, moment by moment.

Reflecting on constant change or impermanence is not a pessimistic notion, but rather facing reality head on. Realizing that no one is exempt can be liberating. Developing the skills of Mindfulness and equanimity can help you not only survive difficult times, but experience deep growth and freedom by helping you gain control of your mind. With this comes a profound level of peace and, as hard as it may seem to believe, deep joy that is free of conditions. You'll soon learn that you don't need things to go your way in order to have the joy that comes from experiencing a deep connection within and to everything around us. This is the only true freedom. This chapter has only scratched the surface of the things that can go wrong. At the end of the day, though, with the application of the right techniques, regular practice, and making Mindfulness an integral part of your life, you can achieve a state of grace and inner peace, and rise above difficult situations.

Chapter 10

Estate Planning

It's hard to imagine, but it's true—one day you'll be gone. There are two major financial areas that should be addressed before your death: replacing your financial contribution to the family (through insurance) and your will. Specifics will vary depending on where you live, so be sure to consult the appropriate professional for guidance in these areas. We provide a general guide for you so you can begin to think about how you'd like to structure things.

LIFE INSURANCE

After you're gone, your spouse, children, and the charities you support will miss your financial contribution (oh, and you too, of course). One of the first steps you should take is to estimate how much they'll miss that contribution. Alter your financial plan by changing your date of death to tomorrow. At this point your income will stop, and there will be a tax bill due. You'll see that the family net worth picture rapidly changes—usually for the worse. However, people who have adequate insurance often will see little or no change to the family wealth. If you are concerned that you're underinsured, try running some different scenarios through the financial plan until you find a level of coverage that you're comfortable with.

If you're not working with a financial plan (although, as you already know, we recommend you do) you can quickly go online and search "insurance calculator." You'll find numerous sites that will walk you through a calculation for the amount of insurance you require. Alternatively, you can use the following rule of thumb.

INSURANCE CALCULATION

70% to 80% of your annual net income x the # of years you want to continue to contribute to the family	= _____
Estimated annual education costs x number of children x four years	= _____
Final tax bill	= _____
Mortgage and other debts you would like to pay off at death	= _____
How much you would like to leave to charity	= _____
Funeral costs	= _____
Total	= _____

Less		
Liquid assets in your name only	=	_____
Current value of life insurance	=	_____
Approximate amount of additional insurance required	=	_____

If you are underinsured, we recommend that you contact three agents and ask them to quote and comment on your situation. Take the quotes back to your CFP or planner, or simply go to your financial plan and put in the numbers for each quote, and remember to add the cost of the premiums into the expense side of the plan. While it's important to carry sufficient insurance coverage, you need to ensure that you can (and always will) comfortably make the premium payments.

There are three major classifications of life insurance: term, whole life, and universal. When you meet the three agents ask them to quote on all three types.

Term insurance is the cheapest option available. You simply buy insurance for a set period of time, say 10 years. At the end of the term, the policy continues at a higher premium.

Depending on circumstances, you can let it drop, continue it at the higher premium (based on your new age) until a pre-determined date is reached, or consider applying for a new term policy (again, based on your new age). If you consider the last option, you'll need to go through the underwriting process again, just as you did when you purchased the first policy. Often this is a less expensive option than simply continuing at the higher premium; however, it's important not to cancel the first policy until you're sure you qualify for the new one. Also, be aware of limitations that can arise in the early years of the new policy, such as a suicide clause covering the first two years of the policy.

Whole life insurance is permanent insurance and guaranteed to last for as long as you pay the required premiums. Whole life policies also include a savings component. The premium you pay is usually more than the actual cost of the insurance. The extra is placed into the savings portion. Eventually you may build up enough in the savings so that the premiums can be paid out of that instead of your own pocket. In some cases you can borrow against the savings portion, although you can't simply withdraw all the cash as that may cancel the policy.

Universal insurance is similar to whole life, except that the savings component of the policy is divided into two parts: a savings element, which accumulates cash to be applied against current and future premiums, and an investment element, which accumulates cash for future investment. There can be tax advantages to universal policies.

If the first three agents you approach fail to arrive at a suitable solution that you can afford, then try three more agents. People often buy insurance because they feel that they've taken up the agent's time and therefore owe her something. As long as you're upfront and they know that you will be looking at other solutions and getting other quotes, you should feel under no obligation to buy. Agents are well compensated for the sale of a policy, in part because it's expected that they will prepare more quotes than policies.

Be wary of "no medical required" policies that are often targeted toward retired people as a way to cover final expenses. The payouts are usually small and the premiums are usually high. Make sure to read the terms and conditions carefully; even though no medical is required, in many cases your coverage becomes void if you die from a pre-existing condition.

DISABILITY INSURANCE

Disability insurance is designed to replace a portion of your income—usually from 60% to 80%—in the event that you're unable to work due to illness or injury. There are two types of disability insurance: short term and long term. Long-term insurance typically starts after your short-term coverage runs out. Most people have some sort of disability insurance coverage through the benefits plan offered by their employer, but these plans can often prove inadequate. Talk to three independent agents about your current level of coverage. It's important to consult a professional because this field of insurance is tremendously complex, and it's essential to have appropriate coverage as it can prevent financial disaster.

In Ben Stein's *New York Times* article "The Sales Profession: Attention Must Still Be Paid" (April 25, 2009) he talks about his personal experience with disability insurance. "Many years later, an insurance broker came to call on my wife about disability insurance. I scoffed at him and told him how incredibly unlikely it was that a healthy woman like my wife would ever be disabled. 'Yes,' he said. 'That's what we think, too. That's why it's so cheap and pays so much if she does get disabled.' I bought the policy, and when my wife did get temporarily disabled, it paid off magnificently and we needed it."

CRITICAL ILLNESS INSURANCE

Critical illness insurance (or living benefits) pays the insured (you) a lump sum amount when you contract one of the prescribed illnesses covered by your policy (such as cancer, heart disease, or stroke). As with life insurance, there's an underwriting process that assesses your health prior to the policy being issued. Critical illness insurance can be very useful as it pays out a lump sum, and you can use it any way you wish—to cover family expenses, medical costs, et cetera.

YOUR WILL

Your last will and testament is likely one of the most significant documents you'll ever write. In it you express your wishes regarding how you would like your estate divided after your death. It will have a profound effect on your spouse, children, business partners, and the charities you support. And rest assured, the government will also be looking for its share of your estate.

One of the most important things to take away from this book is that you should use an experienced estate attorney to advise you and to write your will. I can't imagine a case where you wouldn't benefit from the advice of a seasoned professional in this critical area. To make the most of your meeting, be sure to arrive with

- A complete list of assets

- An outline of what you would like to see happen after your death

- Copies of your insurance policies

- A list of trusted people you might appoint as executors to take over the responsibility of running your estate and distributing your assets

Often the job of executor is given to your closest and most trusted relative or friend; in turn they trust you to leave your affairs in decent order. Being an executor can be a time-consuming task, so it's the least you can do. As a mindful investor, always stay up to date on your paperwork. Throw out anything that's old and no longer applies to you. For example, if you have old share certificates littering up your filing cabinet, deposit them to your brokerage account. Your advisor will research them to determine if they have any present value. Otherwise, your executor will waste time trying to determine their value after your death. Also, clean up any small bank or brokerage accounts by consolidating them. At the same time ensure that the original cost bases for your assets are as accurate as possible and backed with documentation (i.e., trade confirmations, brokerage statements, and real property purchase documentation). If you have spent money to improve or renovate your property, make sure that this is also clearly documented. Ask your accountant if he has all of the information necessary to fill out your last tax return, particularly if you have your own business or family corporation. All of this will save time and frustration later on, and can also help avoid costly tax audits.

When choosing beneficiaries, particularly your children, I would advise that in most cases it's best to have an even hand and to divide everything as equally as possible. While it may be tempting to try to even up the financial lives of your children, particularly if one is failing, that's not your role. This often leads to much bitterness between relatives as it can be seen as punishing a successful heir and rewarding an unsuccessful one. And remember that you can't predict the future: today's happy, successful child with the large family and wealthy spouse may soon be a struggling single parent who could have benefitted greatly from a more even-handed bequest from you. Conversely, the poor slacker brother may be on the verge of licensing the most successful computer game in history and becoming fabulously rich. You just never know.

Try not to worry too much about things or make the mistake of trying to control things or people from beyond the grave.

Just do the best you can with what you know right now, and then relax about it. Some years ago I was giving a workshop with an accountant. We were discussing the idea of transferring a cottage into a Family Trust. An audience member commented, "I'll be really worried if the family members start fighting about the cottage after I'm gone." The accountant replied, in his very English manner, "Madam, you won't be worrying about anything after you're gone." Too true.

Updating Your Will

You should consider rewriting or updating your will in the event of the following circumstances. Note that in some of the following situations your will may automatically become invalid:

- Remarriage, separation, or divorce
- Death of a spouse
- Death, incapacity, or unwillingness of an executor to remain on the will
- Death of a named beneficiary
- When your children grow up or marry
- When assets you have bequeathed in your will no longer exist
- When your tax position or net worth changes substantially
- When you decide to gift assets to beneficiaries before your death

If another situation arises that isn't covered by the above list, check it out with your attorney.

Living Wills

A living will is a document that speaks for you in the event that you're still alive, but unable to speak for yourself because of injury or illness. It outlines your wishes in the event that medical technology can increase your life expectancy through extraordinary means. Basically it gives your caregivers an idea of the stage at which you'd like them to "pull the plug." Make sure you're very specific when detailing your wishes.

In the U.S., the rules governing living wills vary from state to state, and in Canada they vary from province to province. You should consult a legal professional to make sure you have properly expressed your wishes within the limits of the governing laws. Your lawyer can also notarize the document for you, which will help to confirm the validity of the document.

TRUSTS

If you have disabled children or dependent family members, you may need to set up a trust to manage their affairs after your death. Start thinking about who the trustees might be. It's a huge responsibility to ask someone to take on, so you may even want to consider hiring a trust company to run the trust. This option can be expensive, but sometimes employing the professionals is a logical alternative.

Special rules may apply when setting up a trust to benefit a disabled person, so be sure to consult a legal professional in your jurisdiction for more details.

There are many other reasons for trusts, so there are many types. Here are two of the most common ones.

Testamentary Trusts

If you have heirs who are below a certain age (of your choosing; 25, for example), you can set up a trust that takes effect on your death. Assets benefitting the heirs will be held in the trust until they reach the designated age to inherit. In some cases you can set up the trusts so that they distribute income or capital to meet the current needs of the heirs prior to them reaching the age of inheritance. The remaining lump sum of capital is then passed on to them once they reach the specified age.

Trusts often can be expensive to run and may become onerous for the trustees in terms of dealing with the demands of the beneficiaries and the threat of litigation in the event of perceived mismanagement. Be cautious about accepting the role of trustee if you are an individual. While expensive, trust companies are usually better equipped to handle the management of formal trusts.

Spousal Trusts

A spousal trust is most commonly used in the event of a second marriage. Often the person writing the will wishes for their new spouse to receive the benefit of the estate— for example, the income generated from a rental property or investments—but wishes for the assets to ultimately pass along to his children. In cases like these, the assets are held in the trust until the death of the surviving spouse, at which time they are dispersed to the children. As you can imagine, this can be a legal minefield. In some cases, family law statutes will overturn the provisions of such a trust, and can cause massive disruption and loss of tax deferral to the estate. Our advice is to obtain expert legal advice and to proceed with caution.

CHARITABLE GIVING

Our lives are hugely important and, at the same time, insignificant. Lives are short. As Leonard Cohen says, "we are so lightly here." Ultimately, what will be remembered are the lives you've touched. Will you leave the world a little better than you found it? Have you relieved someone's suffering? Have you made a difference when you could?

If you like the idea of leaving some sort of charitable legacy and it's consistent with your personal mission statement, your will or an insurance policy can create a wonderful opportunity for you to make a final act of philanthropy, or allow your estate to establish a charitable foundation in your name.

Giving to charity can be an important way to add purpose to your life. Giving is a real paradox, because when you give, you truly receive. We've all heard that "what goes around comes around" or that "you get back what you put out in the world."

People are wired to give, and many people find their greatest moments of joy come from giving of themselves, whether it be time or money.

In meditation it's taught that when you're stuck in your life and not moving forward, the solution can be giving of yourself. Often this awakens a deep sense that you are connected to something far greater than just yourself, and that one person can make a big difference in the lives of others. The act of giving can change your world and bring you fulfillment.

Giving is an acknowledgement of interconnectedness. This is what a true legacy involves—touching the lives of others, both strangers and people you know. Taking the time to mindfully consider how you'd like to be remembered and how best to provide for your family after you're gone is important. Whether you're in a position to give philanthropically or simply to your family, knowing that you've made the necessary arrangements will give you peace of mind.

Chapter 11

Final Thoughts

Scotland's greatest poet, Robert Burns, was inspired to write these words on a freezing morning in 1785: *"Still, thou art blest, compar'd wi' me! / The present only toucheth thee: / But Och! I backward cast my e'e / On prospects drear! / An' forward, tho' I canna see, / I guess an' fear!"* His plough had just turned over the nest of a tiny mouse, and sent it running into the bitter, cold wind. At that moment he realized that even a mouse in dire circumstances was more blessed than him. The mouse was free and living only in the moment, whereas Burns felt trapped in despair because his thoughts were always focused on the past or the future.

Many people are first drawn to practise Mindfulness by a simple thought—"I can't continue on with things the way they are now." This is certainly an apt description for the state of our economy. Lack of awareness, both internal and external, contributed to recent financial crises. In order to find our way back and regain solid financial footing, we must all endeavour to become more conscious.

While we encourage you to use all of the techniques in this book, you should note that even small changes will have a big impact. Just as a financial plan demonstrates the large impact a small change can have on your finances, simply becoming more aware of yourself and what's going on around you will have a large impact on your life. Even just taking a deep breath and steadying yourself before making a difficult phone call or decision will benefit you. You'll be more centred, relaxed, and aware of what's happening.

As we've said, our goal in writing this book is to help you find greater fulfillment and experience less suffering in your personal, professional, and financial lives. Implementing the strategies in our book will improve your health, lower your stress levels, and make you calmer and more focused. When you apply this calm, focused energy to planning your finances, you'll be able to clarify your goals and be open and honest with yourself about what you're willing and able to do to achieve them. This book isn't about escaping reality, it's about escaping *into* reality. When you face the reality of your situation, focus on your true goals, and apply equanimity to your situation, you'll be well on your way to achieving both inner peace and financial security.

Making Decisions with Mindfulness

Making decisions with Mindfulness is a practical way to bring Mindfulness training into your daily life. You make countless decisions as you move through life, some made in less than a second and others made over years. With the following technique, you'll learn to apply Mindfulness to this process.

The primary purpose of this technique is *to use decision-making as a Mindfulness builder*, while the secondary purpose is *to make better decisions*.

The process of making decisions with Mindfulness described here, which was developed and written by Soryu Scott (see www.budsa.org/decision), has four steps: Define, Explore, Allow, and Launch. These can be easily recalled with the acronym DEAL.

DEFINE

To *define* means to determine a simple representation of the decision in the three subjective spaces—Feel, Image, and Talk. The purpose of this first step is to merely clarify what the decision is in terms of how each of your choices is represented as Feel, Image, or Talk. This allows you to know what you're going to focus on and, of equal importance, what you're not going to focus on. Often the simple process of defining the choices with regard to each of the three subjective spaces is a profound experience.

EXPLORE

To *explore* means to enthusiastically investigate all sides of the decision in each of the three subjective spaces for a period of time, beginning with the definition as you established it in step one. The purpose of this is to create, or figure out, a full and balanced decision you're happy with.

ALLOW

To *allow* means that you go to each of the three subjective spaces in turn to invite that space to contribute to the decision, and then wait patiently, without trying to get anything in particular to come. In this way, you're open to unknown internal knowledge that will help you awaken to a good decision. You can observe the spaces in their active or restful condition. Simply bring the original definitions to their respective spaces, and attend to the space with no concern about what may arise. If a decision comes, or if you've already got one, and it's sufficiently confirmed, use it to launch yourself forward.

LAUNCH

A decision may have come. To *launch* yourself into your decision, begin by maximizing the enjoyment of the decision by focusing on Pleasant Feel. As we indicated in chapter 3, Pleasant Feel refers to pleasant sensations in the Feel space, such as the sensation of your face when you smile. You should allow yourself to experience roughly as much Pleasant Feel regarding the decision as you experienced anxiety, frustration, or concern before you made it. This is a way to encourage yourself to get satisfaction out of making decisions, and to integrate the decision into a positive view of your future. With a positive initial experience, it's easier to begin a course of action that will make the decision a reality.

If a decision hasn't come out of this process, launch yourself into one of three other forward directions:

1. Go back to step one and clearly define the decision again. It's possible that it will be defined differently this time.

2. You may realize that you need more information about the options. Seek this and, once it's acquired, return to step one.

3. You may halt the mindful decision process. In this case, do a focus on Don't Know with an emphasis on equanimity. In chapter 3 we discussed the experience of Not Knowing and remaining comfortable with that. As with all of the techniques from chapter 3, you should aim to apply equanimity to whatever arises, whether it

be pleasant, unpleasant, or confusing. Doing this will guarantee that your time has been well spent, even if there's still no decision.

One of the most important skills associated with this practice is the development of equanimity with regard to Not Knowing. Being uncertain about what to do can make you uncomfortable, but the application of equanimity to this state of mind is ultimately more useful than any one decision, since you don't know everything. To cultivate equanimity within confusion is deeply healthy for the mind, as is the cultivation of Pleasant Feel within certainty.

See the flow chart below for further clarification.

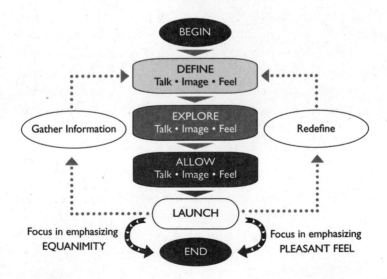

As an example, let's imagine a person using this process. Clarus Kent has moved and now lives a little farther from work. He is deciding if he should buy a car. He doesn't have a car and doesn't want a car, but he also doesn't want to be late, tired, or rained-on when he gets to work via his bicycle. He sits down and uses the decision-making algorithm to figure out if buying a car is the best thing to do.

He defines his possible courses of action. He ignores all but two courses of action, as follows: "I will buy a car," and "I will not buy a car." *Okay*, he thinks, *that was Talk space. Now for Image space.* He directs his attention to Image space in order to find a simple representation of the decision there. He sees himself with a car, and then he sees himself without a car. Just one simple image for each is enough. *All right, that only took about 20 seconds*, he thinks, *now for Feel space.* He knows that he just needs to find the simplest clear representation of the courses of action in Feel space. He directs his attention there, and finds excitement mixed with anxiety regarding buying a car, and a mix of relief, stress, and tightness regarding not buying one. *Great*, he thinks, *in less than two minutes, I have finished the first step, and I already have discovered a lot I didn't know about this decision.*

He then explores these courses of action. He just works with the definitions, continuing to think and feel. He spends about five minutes talking through the decision in his head, and another five minutes imagining scenarios that may occur in each of his two courses of action. He spends about three minutes using the Talk and Image he has explored to bring up Feel, and considers how he feels as it comes up in simple or complex forms.

Very good, he thinks, *in the past 15 minutes I have clarified my decision a lot. I have determined exactly what two courses of action might be. I have listened carefully to the tapes that have been running through my head, so they finally stopped and I could hear the more meaningful talk underneath. By imagining them in detail, I now understand the situations these two courses of action may cause. I trust my feelings on the matter, and understand what ideas these feelings are associated with, and therefore why I feel that way. Now let's move on.*

He then allows the spaces to do the work for him. He is surprised to find that Talk is quiet, except that he hears the words, "It's okay." Image space is blank, but flowing a little and that helps him to relax. Feel is very powerful, and it assures him that he will not drive too much like he used to. This process takes a total of five minutes. *Very interesting*, he thinks, *the past 20 minutes have been very productive.*

He realizes that he is going to buy a car, and that he will track carefully how much gas he uses and how far he drives versus bikes each month. In that way, he gets the best of both worlds, and increases self-awareness and control of his life. He launches himself into this decision by immersing himself in good Feel about it.

He then researches what car to buy on the Internet. He uses the decision algorithm again, and realizes that he needs to gather more information. He sees clearly what he needs to know before making the decision, and launches himself forward by acquiring that knowledge.

He returns to the process, choosing between two cars, an Aquus and a Begwa. Talk space is very clear that the Begwa is the better car even though it is used, but Feel is against it. He can't find a decision, so he drops into equanimity regarding the confusion, and then goes out for a test drive. The drive of the Begwa is great, and he decides that Talk is the way to go this time. He agrees on a price with the dealership, and then at the last moment, Feel becomes Begwa-phobic. He feels a clutching in his chest and doesn't go through with the deal. He leaves, embarrassed but confident due to the equanimity he has developed regarding his confusion.

He uses the process again and discovers that Feel is more clear than Talk, so he stays with his decision against the Begwa. After deeply immersing himself in good Feel regarding his final decision, he purchases the Aquus. He is happy with his car. It turns out to fit his situation even better than he had thought it would.

But now Talk won't let him go. His Feel tells him to forget about the Begwa, but Talk keeps yapping away that there is value in it. He uses the algorithm again, and goes through several iterations of the definition, returning to the beginning to redefine again and again before realizing that the correct definitions in Talk space are, "I am finished with the Begwa," and "I am not finished with the Begwa." He then goes through the process with the second definition even though it seems crazy to not be finished with it.

He remembers that his sister mentioned that she wanted a new car. How did he forget? He is grateful that he didn't get attached to certain definitions, but just took a pair at a time until the correct pair presented itself.

He calls his sister, and she gets excited. Her car is old; it gets terrible gas mileage and she is ready for something smaller. She comes into town to test-drive the Begwa he found. Afterwards, she tells him that during the test drive, it started to make a strange sound. She brought it to a mechanic, and he found something wrong with the engine—a few thousand dollars wrong, in fact. She is shocked, and returns it to the dealer with a sharp complaint. She asks her brother if he had heard the same sound. He says that he didn't hear it, but something in him felt it. Again, he is astonished at the value of the equanimity he cultivated regarding his subjective experience.

They both agree that Begwa is a good make, though, and she soon finds a better one, which she buys and is happy with. *Wow*, he thinks. *Due to careful and systematic decision-making, I got what I needed, and my sister got what she wanted. I did a great job.*

Appendix B

The Budget

Ah, the dreaded b-word: budget. Doing your budget can seem a bit of a chore; however, as we discussed within the main part of the book, it's a critical part of a successful financial life as it can reveal problems, drive your investment and lifestyle choices, and give you the confidence to enjoy the money in your discretionary spending zone (fun money). A budget doesn't have to be a punitive or restrictive thing. After all, it's only a tool. We're just suggesting that you write down your income and expenses for a period of time so that you can become more aware of any problems or opportunities that exist.

Budgets can be useful in revealing lifestyle choices that can be changed. Perhaps reviewing your budget might reveal that if you stop smoking, you can save enough to afford to take your dream vacation, or that you could trade eating out and fast food for a shorter work week. You might surprise yourself and discover that you're really not spending enough, because you are being held back by lack of information and a fear of running out of money.

Being mindful is all about facing reality and finding ways to come to terms with and improve your life. Start your budget with this intention. List three things you would like to do, but aren't sure you can afford. For example:

- An annual, worry-free vacation
- A gym membership or a more expensive, healthier diet
- Working fewer hours
- An annual spa trip
- A new car every four years
- A bigger house
- A revised savings level
- Dinner with friends once a week

This way you'll have an enjoyable thing in mind while creating your budget, and will be more inspired to find ways to reduce your expenses so you can reach your goal.

BUDGET

Incomes	
Salary	
Pension	
Dividends	
Interest	
Business (net)	
Total Income	

continued on page 184

continued from page 183

Deductions	
Work-Related Expenses	
Income tax	
Work travel	
Daycare expenses	
Work clothing cost	
Work-related dining and fast food	
Net Income	
Household Expenses	
Rent	
Condo fees	
Mortgage	
Property taxes	
Sewer and water	
Hydro	
Cable	
Telephone	
Gas	
Cleaning and lawn services	
Maintenance and repairs	
Mobile telephones	

Computer/online services	
Insurance	
Alarm monitoring	
Pool maintenance	
Furniture	
Food	
Groceries (regular)	
Special occasions/holidays (annual/12)	
Snacks, coffee, candy	
Entertainment	
Books	
Magazines/newspapers	
Dining out, movies, theatre	
Alcohol/other	
Tobacco	
Lottery/gambling	
Vacations	
Kids'/grandkids' sports	
Membership dues: tennis/squash/golf/other	
Club food/beverage/guest fees	
Sports equipment	
Sport/travel	

continued on page 186

continued from page 185

Miscellaneous	
Kids' camps	
Kids' allowance	
Gifts/cards	
Pets (food/vet/pet insurance/toys/kennel/travel)	
Drug/medical/dental plan	
Out of pocket medical/dental expenses	
Vitamins	
Massage/physiotherapy/health club/pilates/yoga	
Therapy	
Clothing/Appearance	
Adult clothes	
Kids' clothes	
Haircuts	
Pedicures/manicures	
Makeup/toiletries	
Financial	
Life insurance	
Disability insurance	
Critical illness insurance	

Savings	
Donations	
Accounting/legal/advisory fees	
Consumer interest costs (credit card, LOC, student debt)	
Education	
Private school fees	
Continuing education	
College fees	
Automobile/Travel	
Car loan(s)	
Monthly lease cost(s)	
Insurance (all cars)	
Maintenance	
Gas	
Tolls, parking	
Subway, bus, rail pass	
Other	
Second property additional expenses	
Child support/alimony	
Other	
Total expenses	

Deduct your total expenses from your total income. This will be your surplus (or deficit). Now that you've got everything written down and organized, you can start thinking and planning properly. Some questions that can commonly arise are:

- Do we need two cars?

- After carefully reviewing work expenses and income taxes, is it possible for me or my spouse to retrain for a more personally fulfilling career, even if it generates less income?

- Does it make sense to live the country club lifestyle? Can we afford to live the country club lifestyle?

- Can we really afford private school for the kids?

- Now that we can afford to (fill in the blank), should we?

As you worked through the sheets, questions and issues probably arose. Take your time to think about and discuss them calmly and mindfully. A budget can be a pain to prepare and some of the decisions that have to be made afterward can be uncomfortable, but in the end it's worthwhile. In fact, it's crucial for your financial future.

Finding a Mindfulness Teacher

As we discussed in chapter 8, if you choose to work with an advisor, finding the right one is a critical contributing factor to your potential financial success and peace of mind. Likewise, if you choose to work with a Mindfulness teacher, you will want to give serious consideration to the following questions:

- Is the individual well trained? Who has he studied with? Who has trained and authorized/encouraged him to teach? This will give you a sense of the quality of his training and credibility.

- Does she teach scientifically proven techniques? This will ensure that success can be replicated.

- Does he continue to work with a teacher of his own? This will give you a sense of his ongoing commitment to his own development.

- Does she have professional or life experience that is relevant to you? This will ensure that she can coach you in ways that will enable you to apply the teachings to both your life and your business/profession.

- Who are his students? Do others speak highly of him and recommend him to their colleagues or friends? There's no greater endorsement than a referral.

- Is there good chemistry between the two of you? Do you feel you can learn from this person? You are more likely to learn from someone you understand easily.

- Is she available to you when you need support? Can she tailor the practice to your particular needs? One size does not fit all; within generic techniques there is much leeway and potential to adapt to individual needs.

- Is his aim to help you be successful and develop in your practice? Or does he try to control you in subtle, and not so subtle, ways? Is he encouraging and does he empower you? A teacher should never create a dependency. His goal should be to help you help yourself by developing the skill of Mindfulness.

- Is there evidence that she lives and works in a mindful way? Does she practise what she teaches? And does she have a regular practice of her own?

- Is he ethical and does he exhibit integrity?

The answer to all these questions should be a resounding "yes" because the relationship with a teacher is very important. The right teacher for you will enable you to develop a deep and fulfilling practice and to experience positive transformation in your personal and professional life.

Endnotes

CHAPTER 1

[1] Timothy F. Geithner and Lawrence Summers, "A New Financial Foundation," *Washington Post*, June 15, 2009.

[2] Barack Obama, interview, *Wall Street Journal*, June 16, 2009, <http://blogs.wsj.com/washwire/2009/06/16/transcript-of-obamas-interview-with-the-journal>.

[3] Ibid.

CHAPTER 2

[1] Shinzen Young, "Why Practice Mindfulness?" 2006, <www.shinzen.org>.

[2] Marc Kaufman, "Meditation Gives Brain a Charge, Study Finds," *Washington Post*, January 3, 2005.

[3] Ibid.

[4] Shinzen Young, "Purpose and Method of Vipassana Meditation," 2007, <www.shinzen.org>.

[5] Ibid.

[6] Ibid.

[7] Herbert Benson, *The Relaxation Response*, Avon Books, 1975.

[8] Stephen Covey, *The 7 Habits of Highly Effective People* (Fireside, Simon & Schuster, 1989).

9   Michelle Conlin, "Meditation: New Research Shows that It Changes the Brain in Ways that Alleviate Stress," *BusinessWeek*, August 30, 2004.

10   Ibid.

11   *HR Voice*, October 2007.

12   Shinzen Young, "What Is Mindfulness?" 2007, <www.shinzen.org>.

13   Christopher R.K. MacLean, Kenneth G. Walton, Stig R. Wenneberg, Debra K. Levitsky, Joseph P. Mandarino, Rafiq Waziri, Stephen L. Hillis, and Robert H. Schneider, "Effects of the *Transcendental Meditation* Program on Adaptive Mechanisms: Changes in Hormone Levels and Responses to Stress After 4 Months of Practice," *American Journal of Cardiology*, November 1996.

14   Andrew W. Saul, Ph.D, "Prescription for a Happy Heart," *Vitality*, February 2006.

15   Sharon Begley, *Train Your Mind, Change Your Brain* (Ballantine Books, 2007).

16   Corey Criswell and Andre Martin, *10 Trends—A Study of Senior Executives' Views on the Future*, a Centre for Creative Leadership Research White Paper, 2007.

17   Michelle Conlin, "Meditation: New Research Shows that It Changes the Brain in Ways that Alleviate Stress," *BusinessWeek*, August 30, 2004.

18   Barry Boyce, "Two Sciences of Mind: Cutting-Edge Science Encounters Buddhism's 2,500-Year Study of the Mind," *Shambhala Sun*, September 2005.

19   Charles N. Alexander, Gerald C. Swanson, Maxwell V. Rainforth, Thomas W. Carlisle, Christopher C. Todd, and Robert M. Oates Jr., "Effects of the Transcendental Meditation Program on Stress Reduction, Health, and Employee Development: A Prospective Study in Two Occupational Settings," *Anxiety, Stress and Coping International* 6 (1993): 245–262.

[20] Michelle Conlin, "Meditation: New Research Shows that It Changes the Brain in Ways that Alleviate Stress," *Business Week*, August 30, 2004.

[21] Maria Gonzalez, "Organizational Health: A Strategic Imperative for Sustainable Performance," McGill University, Montreal, November 4, 2005.

[22] Virginia Galt, "Out of the Shadows: Mental Health at Work," *Globe and Mail*, March 29, 2006.

CHAPTER 3

[1] Shinzen Young, "Purpose and Method of Vipassana Meditation," 2007, <www.shinzen.org>.

[2] Shinzen Young, *The Science of Enlightenment, Teachings and Meditations for Awakening Through Self-Investigation*, Sounds True Audio Learning Course, 1997.

[3] Steve Lohr, "Slow Down, Brave Multitasker, and Don't Read This in Traffic" *New York Times*, March 25, 2007.

[4] "Texting Increases Crash Risk 23-Fold: Study," July 28, 2009, <www.cbcnews.ca>.

CHAPTER 8

[1] All of the strategic alliance information in this section is based on Maria Gonzalez's article "Strategic Alliances: The Right Way to Compete in the 21st Century," published in the *Ivey Business Journal*, September/October 2001.

Bibliography

Alexander, Charles N., Gerald C. Swanson, Maxwell V. Rainforth, Thomas W. Carlisle, Christopher C. Todd, and Robert M. Oates Jr. "Effects of the Transcendental Meditation Program on Stress Reduction, Health, and Employee Development: A Prospective Study in Two Occupational Settings." *Anxiety, Stress and Coping International* 6 (1993): 245–262.

Begley, Sharon. *Train Your Mind, Change Your Brain* (Ballantine Books, 2007).

Benson, Herbert. *The Relaxation Response* (Avon Books, 1975).

Boyce, Barry. "Two Sciences of Mind: Cutting-Edge Science Encounters Buddhism's 2,500-Year Study of the Mind." *Shambhala Sun*. September 2005.

Conlin, Michelle. "Meditation: New Research Shows that It Changes the Brain in Ways that Alleviate Stress." *Business Week*. August 30, 2004.

Covey, Stephen. *The 7 Habits of Highly Effective People* (Fireside, Simon & Schuster, 1989).

Criswell, Corey, and Andre Martin. *10 Trends—A Study of Senior Executives' Views on the Future*. A Centre for Creative Leadership Research White Paper. 2007.

Galt, Virginia. "Out of the Shadows: Mental Health at Work." *Globe and Mail*. March 29, 2006.

Geithner, Timothy F., and Lawrence Summers. "A New Financial Foundation." *Washington Post*. June 15, 2009.

Gonzalez, Maria. "Organizational Health: A Strategic Imperative for Sustainable Performance." McGill University, Montreal. November 4, 2005.

———. "Strategic Alliances: The Right Way to Compete in the 21st Century." *Ivey Business Journal*. September/October 2001.

HR Voice. October 2007.

Kaufman, Marc. "Meditation Gives Brain a Charge, Study Finds." *Washington Post*. January 3, 2005.

Lohr, Steve. "Slow Down, Brave Multitasker, and Don't Read This in Traffic" *New York Times*. March 25, 2007.

MacLean, Christopher R.K., Kenneth G. Walton, Stig R. Wenneberg, Debra K. Levitsky, Joseph P. Mandarino, Rafiq Waziri, Stephen L. Hillis, and Robert H. Schneider. "Effects of the *Transcendental Meditation* Program on Adaptive Mechanisms: Changes in Hormone Levels and Responses to Stress After 4 Months of Practice." *American Journal of Cardiology*. November 1996.

Obama, Barack. [interview] *Wall Street Journal*. June 16, 2009. <http://blogs.wsj.com/washwire/2009/06/16/transcript-of-obamas-interview-with-the-journal>.

Saul, Andrew W., Ph.D. "Prescription for a Happy Heart." *Vitality*. February 2006.

"Texting Increases Crash Risk 23-Fold: Study." July 28, 2009. <www.cbcnews.ca>.

Young, Shinzen. "Purpose and Method of Vipassana Meditation." 2007. <www.shinzen.org>.

———. *The Science of Enlightenment, Teachings and Meditations for Awakening Through Self-Investigation*. Sounds True Audio Learning Course. 1997.

———. "What Is Mindfulness?" 2007. <www.shinzen.org>.

———. "Why Practice Mindfulness?" 2006. <www.shinzen.org>.

Index

Page numbers in italics refer to graphs, charts and tables. Page numbers in boldface refer to definitions.